THE SOFTBALL PITCHING EDGE

CHERI KEMPF

HUMAN KINETICS

Library of Congress Cataloging-in-Publication Data

Kempf, Cheri, 1963-
    The softball pitching edge / Cheri Kempf.
      p. cm.
    Includes index.
    ISBN 0-7360-3825-6
      1. Pitching (Softball)   2. Softball for women.   I. Title.
    GV881.4.P57   K46   2002
    796.357'8--dc21   2001051676

ISBN: 0-7360-3825-6

Developmental Editor: Leigh LaHood; **Assistant Editor**: Kim Thoren; **Copyeditor**: Robert Replinger; **Proofreader**: Joyce Raney; **Indexer**: Betty Frizzéll; **Graphic Designer**: Nancy Rasmus; **Graphic Artist**: Sandra Meier; **Photo Manager**: Les Woodrum; **Cover Designer**: Jack W. Davis; **Photographer (cover)**: Tom Roberts; **Photographer (interior)**: Jed DeKalb, unless otherwise noted; **Art Manager**: Carl D. Johnson; **Illustrator**: Tom Roberts; **Printer**: United Graphics

Human Kinetics books are available at special discounts for bulk purchase. Special editions or book excerpts can also be created to specification. For details, contact the Special Sales Manager at Human Kinetics.

Printed in the United States of America

10 9 8 7 6 5 4 3 2 1

Human Kinetics
Web site: www.humankinetics.com

United States: Human Kinetics
P.O. Box 5076, Champaign, IL 61825-5076
800-747-4457
e-mail: humank@hkusa.com

Canada: Human Kinetics
475 Devonshire Road Unit 100, Windsor, ON N8Y 2L5
800-465-7301 (in Canada only)
e-mail: orders@hkcanada.com

Europe: Human Kinetics
Units C2/C3 Wira Business Park, West Park Ring Road, Leeds LS16 6EB, United Kingdom
+44 (0) 113 278 1708
e-mail: hk@hkeurope.com

Australia: Human Kinetics
57A Price Avenue, Lower Mitcham, South Australia 5062
08 8277 1555
e-mail: liahka@senet.com.au

New Zealand: Human Kinetics
P.O. Box 105-231, Auckland Central
09-523-3462
e-mail: hkp@ihug.co.nz

To my brother, who made me want to be a ballplayer
from the very beginning

CONTENTS

PREFACE

I have been a ballplayer for as long as I can remember. Fortunately for me, I had a brother who was three and a half years older than me and had already established himself as a ballplayer before I ever arrived. Throughout my entire childhood, I tried to catch up to him—to hit as far, to run as fast, to throw as hard, and to make spectacular plays we pretended were always necessary.

At first, organized leagues for girls did not exist, so I just hung out at the ballpark where my brother played. I would wait somewhere, strategically, so that I could chase down every foul ball and throw it back in over the backstop. Without fail I would hear someone shout out, "Sign her up!" Eventually at age nine, I signed up to play in my first girls softball league, a division of Little League boys baseball.

I guess it was somewhat accidental that I became a pitcher (in leagues the coach looks for anyone who can get the ball near the strike zone), but from the very start pitching fit me, and it instantly became part of me. Pitching was the spotlight position, the place where all the action was. The position was a showcase for confidence and leadership. Pitching offered the opportunity to succeed or fail every time I let go of the ball. Back then I saw it only as an opportunity to succeed. I loved the speed of the ball, the satisfaction of the strikeouts, and the thrill of winning.

I grew up in softball. True competitive travel ball began with my 13–15 Citizen's State Bank summer team. I moved on to the world-renowned Raybesto's Brakettes Women's Major team and finally to the United States National Team. My skills developed through experience in my backyard and on the streets, learning from mistakes and trying to figure out the best way to get results from the softball. Trial and error, a few tips from people here and there, and one book, *Winning Softball* by Joan Joyce and John Anguillaire, were my resources. Until I was 12 years old, I was the only girl I knew who lay in bed and thought about strikeouts and championships.

Today, millions of young girls lie in bed and think about strikeouts, winning gold medals, and even playing professional softball. Private training is on the rise because children today do not spend endless hours playing street ball and sandlot pickup games to learn the ins and outs of what works and what doesn't. Coaches, teachers, and lessons are supposed to provide all that experience. Twenty-five years after I played in that first league, I have become one of those teachers who, for 30 to 60 minutes per lesson, teach hundreds of eager athletes the sport of softball, specifically the art of pitching. I am not quite sure how I arrived at my profession, but just as the game did so many years ago, it just fit and is now a part of me.

Unfortunately, at times I feel like that eight-year-old without a league in which to play. The teaching of fastpitch pitching has traditionally been done by people who rely on their own perceptions about what happens within the motion. These ideas have largely been those of men who remembered or thought about how they used to do it and passed on these methods by memory or with a frozen shot photo here and there. The physical disparity between a 40-year-old, six-foot-plus, 200-pound male and a 10- to 23-year-old female has rarely been part of the presentation.

Other instructional methods have relied on parallels to baseball pitching and translations of biomechanical data that may or may not have been correct. So-called instructional videotapes now available teach and reinforce almost anything a pitcher has ever done. The truth is that there is a correct way to deliver the ball in a fastpitch motion from the rubber to the plate to maximize effectiveness and minimize risk of injury. The goal of this book is to demonstrate those methods and fundamentals, which are based on biomechanical breakdowns of human movement performed by the most advanced biomechanical laboratories in the country. For the first time, you will see a complete dissection of the pitching motion through photos and drawings of the correct mechanics, based on the work of those motion-analysis laboratories.

As I travel and speak throughout the country, I visit with hundreds of people hungry for information about softball, specifically about pitching. These people are loaded with great intentions of helping young athletes perform to the best of their potential or are themselves pitchers eager to improve. I wrote this book for them. As teachers, we have a responsibility to provide information based on the most modern technology and resources available. It is time to be sure that we back up our good intentions with substantiated, scientific, and practical information.

ACKNOWLEDGMENTS

I would like to acknowledge the American Sports Medicine Institute (ASMI) and specifically Glenn S. Fleisig, PhD, in Birmingham, Alabama; the Belmont University physical therapy department and motion analysis lab—specifically Kevin Robinson, assistant professor; and Tom House and Bio-Kinetics Research and Development. Thanks to Middle Tennessee State University and Millennium Park, Mt. Juliet, Tennessee, for the use of their softball fields for photos. Thanks to all Club K students past and present who have been a part of the ongoing research over the past 10 years. Thanks also to Leslie Barron, Jennifer Wright, Kim Dunlap, Jennifer Brewington, Lindsey Howard, Gaye Lynn Wilson, and Doreen Denmon for modeling in and helping with the photos. And finally, thanks to my editor, Leigh LaHood, for her endless patience with a rookie author!

INTRODUCTION

The fundamentals of pitching are the staple of reliability for a pitcher's long-term success. And although it is often a difficult thing to do, it is important to anticipate competition that will require pinpoint accuracy and high percentages of pitch execution—competition that will pounce on mistakes and quickly turn them into hits and runs. This competition and these hitters are out there, waiting patiently for the challenge of the battle and the opportunity to win.

To meet their challenge effectively, pitchers must be armed with speed, movement, and high levels of accuracy. Equally as important is the pitcher's ability to stay effective season after season (as she climbs through age and ability levels), as well as her ability to stay healthy enough to perform at her peak. Even top college pitchers, pros, and Olympians must remain focused on the fundamentals that will be the foundation of their success, day in and day out. The truth is that close attention to detail is probably what brought about their progress in the first place. By maintaining a solid base and diligently emphasizing small and sometimes difficult movements, those pitchers can maintain their elite status and continue to climb to a higher level.

Learning, understanding, and mastering correct movements will provide a solid base for the further development of pitchers. There is not a college freshman pitcher on the planet that will not take her share of lumps throughout her first year of college softball. The ability to improve and to continually take your game to a higher level is vital.

Pitchers, parents, and coaches should be striving for the future. Pitching is an ongoing process of learning and developing. It will take many years of practice to develop skills and will require physical and mental maturity to pitch at the top levels. Pitchers, parents, and coaches are often so excited about getting to the "good stuff"—the pitches they perceive to be the strikeout pitches and career makers—that they overlook the "little stuff." But in the long run, it is the little things that will make or break a pitcher.

I have often been told that people appreciate the simplicity and common sense understanding they get from seeing the biomechanical breakdown of the pitching motion. That is the goal of this book: to provide simple, common sense understanding of the fundamental fastpitch motion and the movements required to throw the advanced pitches. Good luck!

PART I
PROPER MECHANICS

Throughout this book you will notice an emphasis on correct fundamentals and basic mechanics. These mechanics, whether they pertain to throwing the ball fast and accurately or to throwing an advanced pitch, are the foundation for the pitcher's success and career longevity. The concept of pitching breaks down to performing an aggressive and sometimes even violent action with precision. To accomplish this contradiction, the pitcher must develop a complex set of skills.

To obtain positive results, the pitcher must become skilled at three basic components of mechanics. First is the need for consistency. If the pitcher expects to have pinpoint accuracy as well as command of movement into a small, defined zone, consistency with body movements is vital. By understanding elements such as stride location and length, release point and follow-through, and posture and balance, we can correct mistakes or repeat success.

Second, because the name of the game is fast, the pitcher must maximize her effort so that she can reach her speed potential. By using total effort, the pitcher will accomplish two things. She will gain strength on a routine basis and push her potential threshold to become faster. Also, by using total effort every time, the pitcher will be able to attain a consistent sense of timing for release points, thus improving her accuracy.

Third, creating practice habits and routines is important in establishing and setting the desired movements. It is one thing to hear, feel, or see instruction on a given technique. It is another thing to make that action a habit. Because it is impossible for the pitcher to review the proper execution of every movement on every pitch, she must create habits to repeat success.

STRIVE FOR CONSISTENCY

If you were to set up a game at a carnival in which you gave participants a small ball and asked them to make a backward circle with their arms as fast

© Associated Press

As demonstrated by Lori Harrigan, pitching involves performing an aggressive action with precision.

as they could, let the ball go, and hit a 17-inch-wide, 3-foot-high target at a distance of 35 to 43 feet, you probably wouldn't give away a whole bunch of teddy bears! The truth is that the whole scenario is not as easy as it is sometimes made to appear, particularly when that box becomes a 6-inch-by-6-inch square at the discretion of the umpire. So, to accomplish this mission of delivering a ball accurately to a target with a fast underhand motion, consistency will be extremely important.

The goal of the pitcher is to do the same thing each time to gain the same successful result. If the pitcher also knows what is supposed to happen with the body and where and when the actions should occur, she can more easily correct mistakes that will crop up from time to time. Having this awareness is just the beginning. To be consistently effective, the pitcher must also respond successfully to many mental demands. In both practice and performance, the pitcher needs to be aware of body movements and pitch results that relate to speed, location, and movement.

Remember also that the only way to gauge speed and hold a consistent speed is to use total effort with each pitch. Repeating total effort is much easier than repeating some percentage of total effort. Accuracy is the pitcher's biggest asset at any level. The ability to throw the ball to a location assumed to be a weakness of the hitter has paved the way to success for many pitchers.

To gain consistency with pitch location, it is necessary to create correct habits in body posture, stride placement, arm circle, and follow-through. To help develop these habits, a power line, or line of force, will be used as a basis for effort, energy, balance, and efficiency. In establishing fundamental skills, precision of body positioning and particular placements is of the utmost importance.

After the pitcher establishes correct habits, her success will rely on that one key ingredient—practice. If you want to be a great free-throw shooter in basketball, you have to shoot a lot of free throws! The same goes for becoming an accurate pitcher. There is no substitute for correct repetition. Pitchers must be willing to work hard by themselves and with themselves—always pursuing perfection on a particular area or problem.

MAKE CORRECTIONS ONE POINT AT A TIME

In learning new skills, patience may be the single most important quality. The pitcher must be patient when working on fundamentals and try to remember how difficult it was when she first tried to rub her stomach and pat her head. She must know that the mind perceives the upper and lower body as separate entities and that each is involved with an entirely different action in the pitching motion.

A circular movement with the arm dominates the upper body. Equally as important for the upper body is overall posture and the ability to maintain it throughout the pitch. The lower body moves linearly, involving an initial stride forward and a powerful drive of the back leg to deliver the total body and create efficiency. It is easy for the circular motion of the arm to dominate the pitcher's attention, making it difficult for her to focus on posture and lower-body mechanics.

In practicing fundamentals, especially early on, the pitcher should try to separate the two actions as much as possible so that she can concentrate on one aspect. For example, when working on the arm circle, follow-through, or posture, she can perform drills on one knee so that her legs do not distract her attention or create bad habits of their own. Conversely, when working on stride and drive moves with the lower body, she can omit the arm circle completely or remove the ball so that her entire focus is on the legs. Anytime the pitcher has the ball in her hand, it tends to draw most of her attention.

One of the biggest mistakes in developing technique is stressing accuracy. Pitchers should throw in a controlled environment (preferably into a net) where accuracy is not important or even perceived. *It is impossible to make form adjustments and control the ball at the same time.*

The pitcher should create the fundamental habits first, then work on control. In making corrections, she should focus on eliminating one problem at a time. By working in this manner, the whole process will be much less overwhelming for the new or inexperienced pitcher or the pitcher who has developed bad habits and is not fundamentally sound.

When working on mastering or correcting a technique, the pitcher should minimize the importance of throwing into the strike zone. This idea applies whether the athlete is a 7-year-old beginner pitching for the first time or a 20-year-old college junior trying to correct a movement that has become a habit and is causing repeated injury. The pitcher should keep in mind the following tips:

It's important to maintain upper body posture through the pitching motion, as Danielle Henderson does here.

- She should abandon control to work on the adjustment. Making the correction may require five minutes of warm-up or several weeks of movement mastery.
- Pitchers should be familiar with props that they can continue to go back to in workouts such as power lines, Spinners and oversized balls, balance beams, netted stations, and so forth.
- By focusing on one correction at a time, pitchers are much more likely to see some immediate success. They should try to remain encouraged by noting aspects that they are performing correctly or even just improving slightly. Doing so will help avoid the tendency to view corrections as overwhelming.
- Some athletes need to hear the corrections repeatedly. Others may need to feel the corrections, and still others must see them. An important goal in training is gaining the ability to self-correct.
- In making corrections, three options are available:
  1. Hearing the mistake or correction. (Example: "You're falling off balance to the right.")

2. Hearing about or creating a trigger to help with the correction. (Example: "Imagine yourself on a balance beam.")
3. Physically forcing the correction. (Example: The pitcher actually stands on a balance beam.)

Sometimes athletes can make adjustments only by using the third option. This circumstance is a negative indication because a balance beam cannot be used during competition—the time when adjustments must be made. The pitcher should aim for being able to correct with oral cues or triggers most of the time.

Another coaching tool for corrections is for the athlete to actually see the mistake or correction through videotape or still shots. This method is discussed throughout the book and is effective if used periodically. The previous scenario, however, pertains directly to the everyday training session, which does not always allow the extensive time required for filming and viewing videotape. Also, this method is much like option 3 in that it is not a practical method for pitchers to make adjustments required during competition.

BE COACHABLE

One of the common requests I receive from parents is to evaluate their child— to assess her skills and answer the question, "Does she have what it takes?" In working with pitchers over the years, I have found the most important quality of an athlete is not natural talent, physical prowess, or even instinctive reactions. Those qualities are wonderful when they come in an athlete who loves the game and desires to excel. *But the most important quality in developing an athlete, particularly a pitcher, is the athlete's ability to make adjustments.*

Pitching requires strategy, assessment, and constant adjustments. The pitcher must adjust to the hitter's stance, her swing, the game situation (score, number of outs, inning, etc.), offensive strategies, the weather, the ground, the ball, and the umpire's strike zone. Pitchers must constantly analyze and adjust, whether in practice or in a game, to what their bodies are doing and consequently what the ball is doing. So a supertalented athlete who is unable to adjust instantly, and perhaps even constantly, will have a difficult time succeeding as a pitcher.

DIFFERENTIATE STYLE AND TECHNIQUE

An important point concerning fundamental learning and development is the difference between style and technique. Often, the characteristic most noticeable about a particular pitcher, such as a windup or a glove slap to the leg, is not technique at all. Such moves are the style of that particular pitcher. Style is often the creation of the pitcher and will give her a certain trademark or unique appearance before, during, or after the delivery.

Sometimes a pitcher's style can distract the batter and work to the pitcher's advantage. Other times, style is simply a way to create momentum or perform another practical function such as recovery into a defensive position. At any rate, style is best developed by the individual athlete, not her coach.

For instance, some coaches teach every pitcher the same windup approach or the same mound presence and appearance. This cookie-cutter approach turns the pitcher into an exact replica of every other student, eliminates individualism, and takes each pitcher away from her comfort zone. One pitcher may feel comfortable with a certain movement. Another pitcher may feel stress or discomfort with the same move. Because style movement is personal preference and not a necessary function like fundamental movement, coaches should let each pitcher create something that fits her.

Ralph Raymond, 1996 and 2000 Unites States Olympic head softball coach, used to refer to a great defensive play followed by a muffed throw to the base as "a quarter play and a nickel throw." I sometimes refer to pitchers as having a quarter windup and a nickel pitch. Pitchers should avoid putting too much attention on their style early on and too little attention toward technique. In addition, they must be sure that the style move will not detract from proper technique. Technique is the steak; style is just the sizzle.

THE FINAL PITCH

Finally, in looking at the concept of pitching, the pitcher must know that fundamental techniques are the foundation on which everything else will be built. If that foundation is solid and sturdy, based on strong discipline with correct mechanics, then building upward will be a natural progression. But if the foundation is shaky, any success that comes should be savored because it will likely be short-lived.

The pitcher must not underestimate the importance of getting things right along the way. Athletes, parents, and even coaches often accept mistakes simply because the pitcher is currently succeeding or winning. More often than not, that pitcher has some natural speed and for the moment can outmatch her opponents. Given time, however, hitters will catch up to her speed. Location and movement will become the elements that determine her success.

A pitcher who has only short-term goals is not willing to take a step backward today to take three steps forward tomorrow. This step backward is sometimes necessary in breaking down fundamental mistakes. Short-term goals are fine, but long-term goals are an absolute necessity.

The pitcher must be sure that her foundation will permit growth and a healthy future. She should understand that improvement sometimes means going backward first. Although a "granny shot" in basketball will score two points, it is not a technique that will take the player to the upper level of competition.

PRE-MOTION PRESENTATION

1

The execution of the intended location and movement of each pitch determines how successful a pitcher will be. Having established the importance of consistency and accuracy, we must remember those goals as we examine raw fundamental movements. If the goal is to have pinpoint accuracy, consistently throwing with total effort from 35 to 43 feet away, the pitcher must be particular and precise with each movement.

This precision begins in the pre-motion phase of pitching. From the outset, the pitcher must use a grip, stance, approach, and posture that will allow her to approach the pitch with a maximum opportunity to execute.

GRIPS

The first step to consistency is the gripping of the softball. The grip will affect particulars such as wrist snap and natural ball movement, not to mention basic comfort and the feel of the ball in the hand. Later, we will look at movement pitches, which will have their own grips, but in this chapter we discuss two grips used primarily for the fastball. A good grip should

- establish a consistent feel for the ball;
- establish a firm but loose hold on the ball, just tight enough to prevent it from slipping off or out of the hand before the intended release point; and
- anticipate any natural movement of the softball itself.

The pitcher should use a grip that will allow the top knuckle of each finger as well as the thumb to be located on or across a seam of the ball. Two common grips that allow this to happen are the horseshoe, also referred to as the two-seam grip (see figure 1.1a), and the C, also referred to as the four-seam grip (see figure 1.1b). The pitcher can accomplish the goal of having the fingers and thumb on the seam with both of these grips while experiencing two very different reactions from the ball itself when delivered.

When released, the fastball should roll directly off the fingertips, creating a downward spin. Released correctly off the end of the fingers, the ball

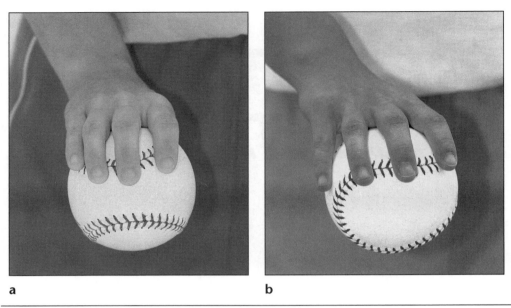

Figure 1.1 Two common grips are *(a)* the horseshoe or two-seam grip and *(b)* the C grip or four-seam grip.

thrown with the C grip will always hold the line on which it was released. For example, if the pitcher releases the ball toward the outside corner of the plate, it will continue on a straight path to that corner without veering or tailing to the right or left. This trajectory occurs because of the four-seam rotation that results when the ball is released off the end of the fingertips. It is important to note, however, that younger pitchers with smaller hands may not be able to reach a seam with the thumb when using the C grip.

On the other hand, the ball released correctly off the fingertips with the horseshoe grip has a tendency to veer or tail on its path to the catcher. Usually, the ball will tail toward the pitcher's throwing-arm side. In other words, a right-handed pitcher will experience a tail or break right, and a left-handed pitcher will experience a tail or break left. The break will not always occur and can vary from ball to ball. The nature and physical makeup of the ball itself creates the movement.

So, with the horseshoe grip, even though the ball is spinning downward, the long seams of the ball moving through the air cause a veering effect. Pitchers often have this type of movement without even realizing it. The good part about this is that sometimes, when throwing fastballs, a little natural movement is a valuable addition to an otherwise straight pitch. However, if a precise target is the goal, the C grip is probably the answer. See figure 1.2 for the different paths of the ball.

Remember that with any grip the pitcher must be able to get the grip with ease, preferably while the ball is in

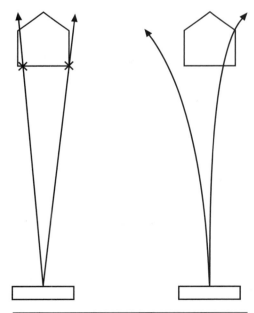

Figure 1.2 Path of the ball with the C grip (left), and possible path of the ball with the horseshoe grip (right).

the glove. Pitchers should keep a ball in hand while watching television or talking on the phone and continue to move the ball around until they are familiar with the path of the seams. They can test themselves by putting the ball behind the back or in the glove and trying to get the grips without looking.

STANCE

Foot placement on the rubber will also be a solid start to consistency. For females in fastpitch softball, the rules are largely the same concerning the approach from the stance. Both feet are required to be in contact with the rubber to begin the pitch (see figure 1.3). Some exceptions to that rule can be found in Little League and high school athletic associations. Initially, coaches should encourage the serious pitcher to abide by the both-feet-on-the-mound method because that style will be required at higher and more competitive levels. It is much easier to go from having both feet on the rubber to having one foot on (when rules allow) than to make the opposite change. Figure 1.4 shows the method of having one foot on the rubber.

The rules also state that the back foot or the foot of the drive leg must always remain in contact with the ground (see figure 1.5). Finally, both feet must remain inside two invisible lines that run perpendicular to the rubber and extend forward and backward from the side edges of the rubber (see figure 1.6). Because the rubber is 24 inches wide, this is known as the 24-inch rule.

Figure 1.3 Both feet on the rubber.

Figure 1.4 One foot on the rubber.

Figure 1.5 The foot of the drive leg must remain in contact with the ground at all times.

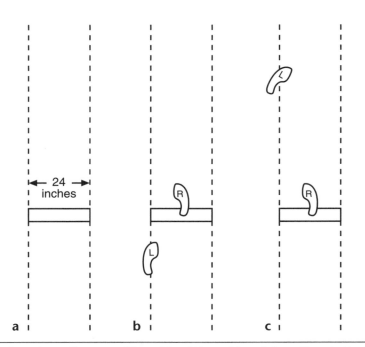

Figure 1.6 Imaginary lines on either side of the rubber *(a)*; an illegal step backward *(b)* or forward *(c)*.

With the rules in mind, the pitcher should place her feet on the rubber to accomplish the goals of creating momentum throughout the pitch and abiding by the rules. The stance should allow some comfort and feed into the common theme of the power line for efficiency and accuracy.

Beginning a violent and aggressive movement by placing the feet evenly together seems awkward and unnatural. So the pitcher should stagger her feet vertically, with the toe of the back foot (or stride foot) on the back edge of the rubber and the heel of the front foot (or drive foot) on the front edge of the rubber (see figure 1.3 on page 9).

Horizontally, the pitcher should separate the feet slightly. According to the rules, the feet can be placed anywhere on the width of the 24-inch rubber. But to create a consistent power line and establish a constant central starting location, the pitcher should locate the front foot (drive foot) in the middle of the pitching rubber horizontally. From there, the back foot (stride foot) can be slightly separated widthwise. A good distance is about hip-width, but remember that the stride foot cannot leak off the outer edge of the rubber.

Some pitchers prefer a much wider stance. Contemplate the wider stance, however, in terms of weight shifting from back foot to front foot (see figure 1.7). With a 24-inch spread between the feet, the pitcher will begin the pitch

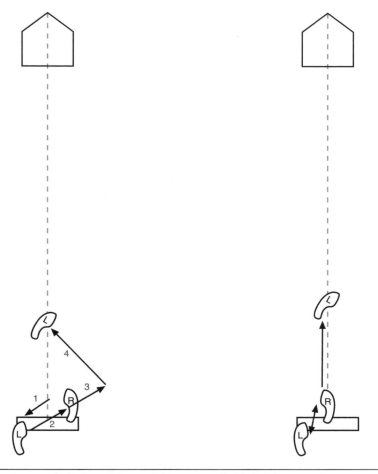

Figure 1.7 Some pitchers prefer a wider stance (left) as compared to a standard stance (right), because of the way the weight shifts.

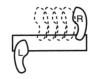

Figure 1.8 The front foot sliding across the rubber.

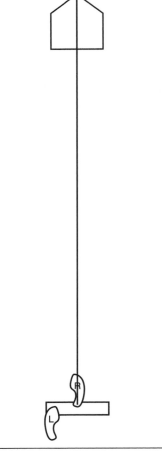

Figure 1.9 The power line runs from the front foot through the middle of home plate.

with momentum moving at an angle *away* from home plate instead of toward it.

Another popular method is to start wide and slide the front foot over toward the middle of the rubber when shifting the weight back (see figure 1.8). This method causes precision mistakes because the pitcher is never quite sure exactly where her front foot stops on the slide. This will prove to be a problem later in the delivery when the stride foot attempts to create the power line to the target. A much safer and substantial method is to place the feet at the beginning of the stance and allow momentum movement only directly back and directly forward.

POWER LINE

In discussing footwork I have referred several times to the *power line*. Let us look a little closer at the overall concept of knowing, establishing, and maintaining the power line. This imaginary line will rule the movements of both the upper and lower body in effective pitching.

The power line, sometimes referred to as the *line of force,* is a straight line running from the pitcher's foot on the front of the rubber directly to the target (see figure 1.9). (We will look at various targets in chapter 5, but for now imagine the target to be located in the middle of the plate.) This line will be the direction for every bit of momentum the pitcher can create—the forward stride of the foot located on the back of the rubber, the arm circle, the drive of the foot located on the front of the rubber, and the consequent delivery of the total body.

In delivering the momentum down the line, an important factor is the pitcher's ability to maintain balance. If the pitcher fails to preserve her balance, energy will be directed off the line of force, thus reducing efficiency. The efficiency of the power line will have a heavy bearing on a pitcher's overall control and her ability to reach her maximum speed.

POSTURE

The last thing to establish in pre-motion is posture. To create maximum speed and consistent height location, the pitcher should stand tall throughout the delivery of the pitch. Some windups will incorporate a bend at the waist to begin momentum. This initial bend, no matter how severe, may aid the pitcher's effort to deliver. But the pitcher must recover from the bend and set a tall and straight upward posture by the time the arm circle begins.

The posture that the pitcher initially sets within the motion will have the spine straight but comfortable and the head directly over or slightly in front of the belly button. Once she sets this posture, the pitcher must maintain it throughout the pitching motion (see figure 1.10).

Any variation of posture that causes a lean or bend forward will affect speed because the pitcher will have to go beyond her most powerful location of release (the bottom of the circle) to get the ball in the strike zone. When a pitcher releases the ball in the power zone with forward posture, the ball will angle downward. To get the ball into the strike zone with forward posture, the pitcher must release a considerable distance past the bottom of the circle, thus reducing overall speed. Younger pitchers often develop forward posture in an unconscious attempt to keep from throwing the ball too high (see figure 1.11).

On the other side of the posture spectrum, if the pitcher tends to lean backward throughout the delivery, the trajectory of the ball will be too high (see figure 1.12). The pitcher with backward posture will tend to throw above the strike zone. Pitchers will need some integrity and body awareness to set the correct posture from the outset and maintain it throughout the motion.

THE FINAL PITCH

This chapter begins our discussion of the fundamentals of the motion. Pitchers and coaches sometimes find it difficult to understand the importance of every movement. But they must realize that any mistake at the beginning of the motion will turn into a larger problem by the end. Coaches should not hesitate to break this down for the new pitcher until she has a good feel and understanding of what is required.

At the outset of learning the mechanics of the stance, stride, and so on, it is important to establish a rubber and power line. The rubber should be regulation size—24 inches long and 6 inches wide. The power line for now should be a straight line that begins in the middle of the rubber and projects straight outward approximately six to eight feet. The power line can be defined with a real rubber; with a taped or painted line; or a drawn, taped, or painted rubber with a taped or painted line.

Many pitchers in their pursuit of perfection are embarrassed about losing control of the softball. A simple wild pitch becomes humiliating. Consequently, pitchers usually adjust their posture, especially by leaning or bending forward, to keep the ball lower and under control. For that reason, when pitchers make posture corrections during the motion, they should remember that they will experience an extreme loss of control high or low. Pitchers should expect that they will throw wild pitches and be receptive to correction of posture or follow-through, regardless of the location of the pitch.

a

b

Figure 1.10 Some windups start with a slight forward bend, but the posture is straight as the arm circle begins and throughout the pitching motion.

c

Figure 1.11 Forward posture tends to reduce the speed of the pitch.

Figure 1.12 Backward posture can result in a pitch above the strike zone.

Furthermore, for the advanced pitcher who may be experiencing performance or health problems, revisiting the breakdown of the pre-motion, or in some cases being introduced to it for the first time, can be a positive and enlightening experience. Many naturally talented pitchers may have gotten away with disregarding details up to a certain point. These natural athletes sometimes have the most difficulty in learning body awareness and proper mechanics if they are not introduced to them at the beginning of their careers.

FEET AND LEGS

2

The primary goal for efficiency in the motion is to get the entire body to agree on the task at hand—to pitch the softball as fast as possible toward a designated target. Sometimes it is easy to allow the arm circle to hold most of the focus and attention because that motion is so dominant. But to obtain efficiency, use the total body, and reduce the chance for injury caused by the unbalanced use of the upper body, it is crucial to get the footwork correct. Mistakes in developing footwork, especially the back-leg drive, are commonly made by pitchers *and* instructors.

STRIDE AND DRIVE

To begin, we have to set the terminology. The leg that is opposite the throwing arm and located on the back side of the rubber in the stance is the stride leg. For example, the stride leg for a right-handed pitcher is the left leg.

The leg located on the front side of the rubber in the stance is the drive leg. This drive leg has traditionally been referred to as the pivot foot; however, to perform the motion correctly, this foot will not pivot but instead lift up and over the top of the toe. Therefore, it is a misrepresentation to refer to the drive leg as the pivot foot (see figure 2.1).

In beginning the motion, the pitcher should shift her weight

Figure 2.1 Drive leg (front) and stride leg (back).

Figure 2.2 The foot landing efficiently at a 45-degree angle on the power line.

Figure 2.3 The foot landing inefficiently straight on the power line.

to the foot located on the back of the rubber, the eventual stride foot. As she begins the circle, she shifts her weight back to front, from the stride foot to the drive foot. The stride should be aggressive and quick, and she should land flat, absorbing her weight on the ball of the foot.

As the foot lands flat, it should be positioned at a 45-degree angle with the ball of the foot located directly on the power line (see figure 2.2). The 45-degree angle of the foot is important for several reasons. First, when the foot lands at the slight angle, the hips and shoulders, if allowed to go along with the stride, will also land at a 45-degree angle. For the shoulders, this foot placement allows the slight upper-body rotation needed to optimize delivery of the ball. The hips will gain the same amount of rotation, allowing for efficient delivery of the lower body.

If the front foot lands exactly straight on the power line, as shown in figure 2.3, the hips and shoulders will be allowed no efficiency with horizontal rotation during the motion. Pitchers who land too square will often tend to cross the body with the delivery or hit the hip solidly with the throwing arm, causing the ball to veer off in the direction of the throwing hand.

If the front foot lands at a 90-degree angle (see figure 2.4), the hips and shoulders will overrotate and the pitcher will end up with no lower-body contribution to the pitch whatsoever. Another more serious problem with the 90-degree landing of the front foot is the unnecessary pressure it applies to the stride knee.

Human movement tells us that the knee is meant to bend forward, not sideways. Yet this type of landing requires the knee joint to accept the force of the stride (two to three times the body weight) while the knee is positioned sideways. For that reason, if the pitcher repeats this mistake, she is more likely to experience serious ligament damage within the knee joint. You will often observe a pitcher with this style wearing some sort of knee brace or support on her stride leg.

Pitchers who overrotate will also tend to throw the ball uncontrollably off to their throwing-arm side until they learn to compensate for the position of their hips.

Now, let us go back to the landing of the ball of the stride foot on the power line. This landing will position the foot (drive foot), toe (stride foot), and target in a direct line (see figure 2.5). As the stride moves forward, the heel of the drive foot should lift up, relieving the weight from that foot. At the landing position of the stride foot, the drive-foot heel should be up and the tip of the toe on the ground, as shown in figure 2.6. This positioning will enable the drive leg to begin its move forward into the pitch immediately after the pitcher sets the stride leg.

Figure 2.4 The foot landing at a 90-degree angle.

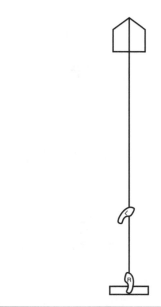

Figure 2.5 The stride foot's land aligns the drive foot, stride-foot toe, and target in a direct line.

Once the stride foot lands flat and is set, the drive leg begins its move forward with the knee of the drive leg heading for the target and directly down the power line. The toe of the drive leg will head toward the heel of the stride leg, leaving a banana-like impression in the dirt (see figure 2.7).

As mentioned before, once the stride foot has landed at 45 degrees, the hips will also set at 45 degrees (see figure 2.8). The pitcher should maintain this angle for the hips throughout the motion until she releases the ball and

Figure 2.6   At the stride-foot landing, the heel of the drive foot should be up with the toe on the ground.

Figure 2.7   The path of the drive foot. Notice the path is straight before the banana due to more glide during the stride.

Figure 2.8   The hips will follow the stride foot's 45-degree angle.

assumes a defensive stance. It is not necessary to talk about the hips a lot because they will take care of themselves if the feet are positioned correctly.

STRIDE LENGTH

Pitchers and coaches often ask how to determine the length of the stride. There is no absolute answer except to say that the stride should stay aggressive and should not exceed a length that would hinder the pitcher from moving the back leg into the pitch comfortably. Likewise, height of the stride is not an absolute but is based on the timing of the front foot being set in relation to the pitching arm. We will discuss this topic in detail in chapter 4. Two facts relate to the positive effect of the stride on pitch speed.

- The quicker the stride leg moves and sets, the quicker the arm will move to maintain timing. Passive pitchers who stride with no energy often match that timing with a slower arm circle.
- The longer the stride, the faster the pitch will *seem*. The hitter's perception of speed equates one foot of distance to about three miles per hour.

To elaborate on the perception issue, if two pitchers throw the same speed but one lands 35 feet from the hitter and the other lands 34 feet from the hitter, the pitcher who lands closer would *seem* to be three miles per hour faster. A radar gun would read the speeds the same, but the hitter's *perception speed* is adjusted.

To increase stride length beyond her height while maintaining efficiency of the back-leg drive, the pitcher must employ a glide method off the drive foot. As the stride leg goes forward and hits a comfortable distance between the stride and drive legs, the drive leg, having lifted weight up and over the tiptoe, will begin to glide forward while the stride foot is still airborne (see figure 2.9). The tiptoes of the drive leg will maintain contact with the ground throughout the glide, keeping the pitch legal.

In the pursuit of excellence, do not compromise body efficiency or balance for a couple inches of stride length. For younger pitchers, good timing and

Figure 2.9 The drive foot glides with the toes on the ground while the stride foot is off the ground.

solid body work should be stressed and established before attempting the longer stride moves.

This gliding method allows the stride leg to reach out farther than it could if the drive leg had stayed set at the pitching rubber. When you hear of a pitcher with an exceptionally long stride, you can usually attribute that to the method of striding and gliding. In working on the longer gliding stride, the pitcher should remember that the distance between the feet and legs stays the same as it would with an aggressive but non-glide stride. The stride does not become wider (feet and legs farther apart); it simply becomes longer (reaches closer to the plate). Once the stride foot lands and sets, the drive leg continues forward normally.

FINISH POSITION AND DEFENSE

The job of the pitcher is to pitch first and then play defense. Pitching and defense are two separate entities, so she should not try to blend them. The pitcher who starts to take the defensive position midway through the motion will rush the hip through and eliminate the 45-degree angle for the hips before completing the motion, thus reducing side-to-side control and efficiency.

The pitcher has an important defensive role. Sharp reactions are helpful because at the completion of the motion the pitcher will often be the closest player to the hitter. Therefore, with all pitches, the pitcher should land in a good defensive position, balanced with the glove in front of the body, as she completes the motion. Ending in this position must be automatic.

You can't have your cake and eat it too. The pitcher is taught to visualize success, to believe in herself and her ability to control hitters. With that in mind, a shot back up the middle should be a total surprise to the pitcher. But if she has finished in good defensive position and has sharpened her reactions through practice, she will defend herself and the position effectively.

Back to the cake. A coach cannot ask a pitcher to visualize one result (strike) but *expect* the opposite result (hit). Therefore, the pitcher should develop and practice a finishing defensive position. Reactions must become automatic.

CATCHING COMMON ERRORS

Let's take a look at some of the common mistakes made with lower-body mechanics:

The drive foot pivots to a 90-degree angle as the stride leg moves forward. The theory behind the "open the door, close the door" method of pitching sounds practical, but the results in large part fail the intentions. This method calls for the pitcher to "open" the hips as far as possible to face 90 degrees away from home plate (with the belly button of a right-handed pitcher facing the third baseman) as the circle goes upward, and to "close" the hips as she throws the ball. In theory this would generate the maximum force available to the body and use the hips to their greatest potential.

The theory is sensible, but the reality is that if the back foot pivots beyond 45 degrees and the knee turns sideways, the back leg will probably not contribute to the motion before the ball is released. The time that elapses during the arm circle is simply not long enough for the drive leg to pivot out and turn back toward the target to drive the leg or hip through the pitch before releasing the ball.

Consequently, the lower body (legs and rear) does not contribute to the pitch. In hanging back, the lower body disconnects the efficient flow of the body by forcing the upper body, specifically the arm, to absorb more of the deceleration phase after release.

In addition, a lagging or nonexistent leg drive will usually cause the head and shoulders to lean forward. This posture will tend to result in the practical problem of inconsistent height location and the health problem of additional strain on the lower back.

Remember the goal of getting the entire body to agree on the task? This mistake of the back foot causes the body to be divided in its goal. Many pitchers who try to drive the back leg after the pivot end up sliding the foot forward with the knee still sideways. This can cause unnecessary wear and tear on the tendons and ligaments of the drive knee as well as the stress on the stride knee that we previously discussed. Videotape of this mistake can clearly illustrate the order of the movements.

Too much weight on the drive foot as the stride foot sets.   This mistake is often characterized by a flatness of the drive foot that seems unable to lift the heel and bend upwards. This action will cause the leg drive to be slow and inefficient in its contribution to the motion. The pitcher should try to start up on her toe more, either by putting her foot in that position or by placing something under her foot to lift the back heel off the ground.

The drive foot flies off the ground, creating an illegal pitch.   This circumstance occurs when the heel of the drag foot lifts up and over, but the force of the stride, the height of the stride, or the pushing of the drive foot against the rubber causes the entire foot to lift off the ground (see figure 2.10).

Figure 2.10   Here the drive foot is off the ground, which is illegal.

Because the back foot must always stay in contact with the ground, this is an illegal pitch. Placing a small piece of paper, about a half-inch wide and three inches long, just in front of the drive foot can help the pitcher learn to keep the foot on the ground (see figure 2.11). In her stride outward, she should drag the piece of paper along the ground as the drive leg comes forward. If she makes the illegal move, the paper will not move.

The pitcher uses a crow hop or pivot, a jump, and a replant, creating an illegal pitch. Coaches and parents sometimes overemphasize the push off of the rubber with the drive leg. When a pitcher habitually pivots and then tries to force her body outward by pushing off the rubber, a crow hop, or replant, of the ball of the foot occurs (see figure 2.12). For this to happen the foot must leave the ground and reset, creating an illegal pitch.

Figure 2.11 Placing a piece of paper in front of the drive foot helps keep the foot on the ground.

To alleviate problems of stride and drive feet, the emphasis must be refocused on lifting the drive-foot heel, causing an upward over-the-toe position and leaving the toe in the dirt, in contact with the ground. The feet must not go beyond 45-degree angles. Also, take a look at the height of the stride leg. If it is exceptionally high, the pitcher should try lowering it slightly.

Figure 2.12 A crow hop, or replant, of the back foot.

She shouldn't shorten the stride length, just lower the height of the stride. The paper drill mentioned earlier is useful with the crow hop, pivot, and replant.

PRACTICE IT

To correct a habitual pivot of the back foot, try placing a ball at the inside of the drive foot (see figure 2.13). If the pitcher uses the correct action, the heel of the drive foot will not disturb the ball. If the pivot occurs, the ball will roll away.

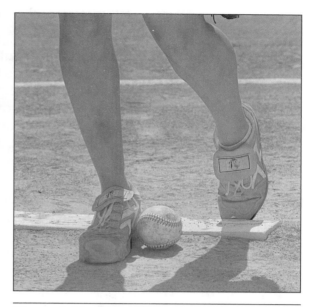

Figure 2.13 Place a ball at the inside of the drive foot to prevent a pivot.

PRACTICE IT

Another drill to correct the back-leg drive is for the pitcher to start about a stride away from the catcher. The catcher places the mitt at the height of the pitcher's knee (see figure 2.14). Without a ball, the pitcher goes through the motion, striding right under the catcher's glove. As soon as the stride foot is set, the drive-leg knee should come forward and into the glove. The toe of the drive leg should still go toward the heel of the stride foot. This drill will create a nice visual aid even when the pitcher is 40 feet away.

Figure 2.14 The knee-in-glove drill.

Missing the power line with the stride leg. Some pitchers inadvertently but consistently step to the right or left of the power line. Pitchers who have this problem can remedy it through repetition, either by performing the motion without a ball or by throwing to a nearby net. In performing this exercise, the pitcher will be able concentrate on stride-foot location without being concerned about the location of the pitch.

The "bowling kick" or "walking through" of the drive foot and leg. Proper movement of the drive foot holds the angle of the body at 45 degrees throughout the motion, helping to stabilize side-to-side control. In addition, by lightly dragging the ground, the drive foot stabilizes balance. Usually, pitchers who kick the foot sideways behind them (the "bowling kick") will fall off balance to the opposite direction. This too will affect side-to-side control.

PRACTICE IT   To help the drive foot come forward correctly, try the "drag the paper" drill mentioned previously. Pitching from a pitcher's balance beam can also help cure these problems by forcing the pitcher to find a way to balance, thus calling up correct toe-to-heel mechanics.

PRACTICE IT   Long tossing a ball is an effective way of uncovering lower-body problems. *Distance will magnify mistakes.* Pitchers can start at regulation distance and gradually back up to 75 to 150 feet, depending on size and strength. As the pitcher backs up, she can put a slight arc on the pitch to carry the distance. This activity should appear more like tossing or playing underhand catch than pitching. The focus should not be on throwing a strike heightwise but on stepping on the power line or pulling the ball through a straight line. In backing up, if the pitcher does not correctly use the back-leg drive, she will compromise her posture and the ball will die short of its destination. This drill can greatly improve the pitcher's understanding of proper mechanics.

Repair of any mistake requires diligent repetition of the correct mechanic. The pitching rubber and power line at home will get lots of use. The pitcher should do sets of 10 repetitions of the correct mechanic, first without the ball and then with the ball. These sets of 10 reps can be spread over the course of an evening with breaks between repetitions. Next thing you know, the pitcher will be able to execute 50 to 70 quality repetitions of the correct movement!

THE FINAL PITCH

Pitchers initially have difficulty focusing on lower-body mechanics. The dominance of the motion, the arm circle, is up top, and pitchers tend to focus on that. Working with shadow pitching (no ball) or in a close proximity to a net will draw attention away from accuracy and toward lower-body mechanics.

Remember that we are trying to make the pitching motion a two-step process:

1. The front side (drive leg, front-side arm circle, and glove) goes forward, and

2. the back side (drive leg and back-side arm circle) comes through.

Any delay of the drive leg turns the motion into a three-step process:

1. Front-side arm circle (drive leg and glove)

2. Back-side arm circle

3. Leg drive

This three-step process produces inefficiency because the release of the ball precedes the drive of the back leg.

A thorough explanation of the two-step process, along with a few visual aids here and there, usually leaves audience members nodding their heads in perfect understanding. Using the effort and energy of the entire body to pitch the softball makes good sense. Still, incorrect footwork is one of the most common mistakes that pitchers make.

ARMS AND POSTURE 3

The action above the waist is dominated by the arm circle itself, but it also involves the crucial aspects of overall body posture, glove-hand positioning, and follow-through after release. Once it begins, the arm circle is often so dominant that pitchers have a difficult time focusing on any other movement. In developing body awareness and learning advanced pitching techniques, the pitcher must eventually overcome undue preoccupation with the arm circle. Still, because of its all-encompassing effect, sometimes over all other body movements, we will first look at the arm circle.

ARM CIRCLE

The center point and obvious focus of the fastpitch motion is the arm circle. Why one person's arm is able to go faster than another's has to do with many factors, including genetics, athleticism, strength, maturity, repetition, and the inevitable factor of God-given talent.

A pitcher who throws the ball 70 miles per hour was born with that ability. No matter how badly we pitching coaches would like to take credit for the speed of a fireball pitcher, the credit belongs to the gene pool and the athlete herself. Each athlete, however, has an individual potential speed of pitching. The responsibility of coaching is to ensure that the athlete reaches her potential and has the fundamental mechanics to maintain a healthy arm throughout her career.

The goal of the circle is to be as quick as possible and to generate as much speed as possible throughout rotation of the arm. To do this, the pitcher must keep two main concepts in mind.

- She must find and establish her natural motion.
- In developing the circle and continuing down the road in developing speed, she must remember that loose muscles are fast and tight muscles are slow.

Let's take a closer look at those concepts.

© Duomo/CORBIS

Michelle Smith demonstrates proper technique for the arm circle—the center point and focus of the fast-pitch motion.

Find and establish natural motion. Natural motion for the arm circle will vary for each pitcher according to body type, strength, and so on. Nevertheless, each athlete should have a natural arm circle that is smooth and uninterrupted. Coaches should refrain from requiring certain locations for arm-circle positioning, such as a particular degree of extension or a brush by the ear. Some absolutes—based on human movement—exist for maximizing the speed of the circle, but the pitcher should be careful not to overanalyze the arm positioning.

Loose is fast; tight is slow. To enhance and maximize speed, the lever, or arm, must be loose. A loose arm allows a whipping motion, especially through the back side of the circle. This action is the key to pitching fast. The tighter the joints (wrist and elbow) and muscles, the less whip the pitcher will gain.

In referring to the pitching arm as a lever, it is true that longer levers are advantageous to speed, but total extension of those levers is unnecessary and often a waste. The advantage to longer levers is the fact that they produce more force in the whip and a greater force in unloading. Think of the old children's game crack the whip, which works better with more people (longer lever). The last person gets slung more aggressively as power transfers from person to person while everyone is skating or running in a circle. The lead person gets ahead, the power transfers through the middle, and the last person finally receives all the built-up energy, which slings her through with great force. Now imagine if the whole line skated together evenly in a straight line. The only force exerted to sling the end person would be a small strength move by the next-to-last person. No energy would be built up and transferred through the line. The arm works as a lever in the same way. The more energy that the arm can build up and unload through the whip, the faster the pitch.

Another way to understand the whip of the arm is to relate the pitch to other athletic movements performed with the levers of the arms or legs. First, take overhand throwing. How odd it would look for an athlete to lock the elbow out, straighten the arm, and then bring the whole thing through at once, straight and rigid. Or imagine a field-goal kicker drawing his leg back, straightening it out, and swinging the leg through as straight as a board to kick the football. In these instances and many others, we know that the middle joint of the lever—the elbow in the overhand throw and the knee in the kick—leads the motion (see figure 3.1). Fastpitch softball is no exception; the elbow leads the arm through the pitching motion.

The natural motion of an athlete with no preconceived notions of how to pitch is usually a loose, smooth circle. To understand this point, the pitcher can try this simple drill. She strides out with the leg opposite the one she usually uses. Using this stride position as a stationary stance, without the glove on, she starts making a backward circle with the glove hand. In other words, a right-handed pitcher would take a stance with her right leg forward and swing her left arm backward.

The pitcher keeps the circle going backward without interruption. She gradually adds speed to the circle. The coach should watch the arm throughout the circle. Because the glove hand and arm have not established any bad

a   b

Figure 3.1 In both (a) an overhand throw and (b) a football kick, the middle joint leads the motion.

habits, this motion is usually an athlete's natural motion. After the pitcher has felt the loose, smooth left arm (and the coach has seen it), the pitcher should repeat the drill with the pitching arm, keeping in mind the same concepts—just spinning the arm and remaining loose, relaxed, and smooth.

To take a closer, more detailed look at the correct mechanics of the natural arm circle, the pitcher should stand with her arms relaxed and down to the side. Most people in this relaxed state will have their palms aimed toward the body. Some people at rest, in a relaxed position, will have their palms aimed slightly backward. The forearms in both positions will rest against their sides (see figure 3.2). Whatever the natural relaxed position is for the pitcher, that is the angle positioning in which the circle should start.

A common analogy is to start the circle with the hand positioned as if you were shaking hands with someone. The circle goes up and around smoothly from that starting position. As the arm moves through the circle, it should always be relaxed with a slight bend, and the middle joint of the lever, the elbow, should always lead the arm down and through the back side of the circle. In moving the arm through the circle, the pitcher need not twist or reposition the wrist. At the bottom of the circle, as the elbow leads past the hip, the wrist will naturally fall into a cocked position. Some pitchers like to turn the ball outward or away from them-

Figure 3.2 People have different resting arm positions: palms aimed slightly backward (left) and palms toward the body (right).

selves as they lift up the front side of the circle, but they must avoid too much forced positioning with the hand. The pitcher should try to start naturally and let the arm and hand swing around as loosely as possible.

The most extended point of the arm will be at the release of the ball. If the pitcher is in her natural motion as the arm circle comes past her body, the forearm will brush slightly past her side (see figures 3.3 and 3.4). This brush is not heavy or harsh, and it causes no interruption to momentum. Remember, at rest, the arm hangs downward with the forearms resting against the side, naturally.

a

b

c

Figure 3.3 If the pitcher is in her natural motion as the arm circle goes past the body, as shown here, the forearm will lightly brush the side.

Glove Hand

Going back to the use of the total-body concept, let us direct our attention to the glove hand. As the circle begins, the glove hand and arm should simultaneously rise with the throwing hand and arm. (If the two are actually in contact with the ball hidden in the glove—bonus!) The glove hand should rise at least as high as the chest and could go as high as the top of the circle before peaking out (see figure 3.5).

When the throwing hand equals that positioning on the back side, both arms should move downward together like a jumping jack. Note also that the glove should be located over the power line and should remain there

Figure 3.4 The forearm lightly brushes the side.

a   b   c

Figure 3.5 *(a, b)* The glove arm rises with the throwing arm. *(c)* The glove can rise as high as the circle.

throughout the up-and-down motion of the arm. Any flying outward with the glove indicates movement away from the target, which will weaken the foundation for advanced pitching.

Follow-Through

After the wrist snap and release of the ball, the hand and arm must follow through to complete the pitch. The correct follow-through will have a positive effect on speed and control and will reduce soreness and the risk of injury to the elbow and shoulder joints.

In the follow-through, the elbow should come past the side of the body but not go above the plane of the shoulder. Ideally, the follow-through, like the circle, stays loose and relaxed. A perfectly natural follow-through has the arm directly extended in front of the body toward the target with the hand pronated or loosely turned downward, with a dangling wrist and fingers (see figure 3.6). Note that the pronation of the wrist downward happens *after* the release.

To work on this, the pitcher should position herself on one knee close to a net. She throws the ball into the net and immediately continues to move the arm outward to reach and grab for the net. The force of the ball will have knocked the net away, but the visual aid is often effective. If this follow-through does not occur naturally, the pitcher may have to force the follow-through a little more mechanically.

In learning a more mechanical follow-through, the pitcher should finish in an L or U position with the bicep or upper arm parallel to the ground and palm facing her head (see figure 3.7). The elbow should never snap tight for the follow-through. Whether close to the side or out in front of the pitcher, the snap is an unnecessary and senseless movement. Over time, the elbow snap will cause undue stress and soreness to the elbow joint.

Figure 3.6 The ideal position of the arm at follow-through.

Figure 3.7 In the L or U position, the upper arm is parallel to the ground and the palm faces the head.

Windup

Now that we have a solid understanding of the goals for the upper body in the delivery, we should back up to the beginning of the motion and look at the windup. As mentioned earlier, the windup is in large part the style of a particular pitcher, but, to go a step further, it truly has two purposes.

- **To distract or intimidate the hitter or legitimize the pitcher.** Everyone has seen an average pitcher with a unique and crazy windup become distracting to hitters. The windup is sometimes effective in that manner, and it may also be intimidating because it adds aggressiveness and confidence to the look of the pitcher. In legitimizing the pitcher, a windup can take a pitcher from a simple, uncomplicated look to a more confident, complex, and advanced appearance.

- **To contribute to the arm circle itself by adding aggressiveness and momentum.** By creating movement before the circle, the motion gives a boost of momentum into the circle. This adds rhythm to the motion as well as comfort to the pitcher, compared to beginning the circle from a dead stop.

The pitcher can choose from among many windups to reach these goals. In choosing one, however, she should keep in mind that the goal of the windup is to contribute to the motion of the arm circle, not detract from it. For example, a windup that begins with the arm locked out straight stands a good chance of detracting from the motion (see figure 3.8). From the mechanics of the circle, we know that the goal is to be loose and fast, so locking the arm initially would work against the ultimate goal. Many young pitchers—especially those who begin the circle with a straight-arm windup—remain straight and locked throughout the circle.

Another example of a style technique that can have a negative outcome is the slap of the leg with the glove. Many pitchers use this glove slap at the beginning or end of the motion as a momentum generator or distraction. The same pitchers often complain of bruises or soreness in the leg. Figure that one out on your own. Some windups do not involve the glove, putting the pitcher into the circle with a "dead" or uninvolved glove hand.

a

b

c

Figure 3.8 If the arm is locked out straight during the windup, it may stay that way throughout the circle.

Male fastpitch pitchers are extremely conscious of hiding the ball from the hitter and the first-and third-base coaches. Most windups that male pitchers use are relatively simple and maintain the theme of hiding the ball until release. Girls, for some reason, tend to be more creative with the windup and less in tune to the idea of hiding the ball. In advanced pitching and upper-level competition, exposing the ball can be a big weakness because coaches and hitters have a chance to check grips. Also, hitters simply get their eyes on the ball sooner, increasing their comfort, confidence, and ability to make contact.

In summary, the windup can be personal and unique, but it should accomplish the goals of the motion along the way. Keep in mind that one key advantage a pitcher has is the ability to hide the ball.

POSTURE: THE BACKBONE OF THE MOTION

A mistake that many pitchers make within the motion is using incorrect or inconsistent posture. Some pitchers simply do not notice the problem; others underestimate the overall importance of posture to speed, control, and the ability to throw movement pitches correctly. We will discuss the latter in subsequent chapters, but in regard to technique, incorrect posture can inhibit speed by changing release points, forcing the pitcher to release beyond the most powerful position for the snap. In relation to control, posture can manipulate the true perception of where the release point would occur if the pitcher's body were in the correct upright position. Unfortunately, the natural focus of the pitcher and parent often goes to the more obvious aspects of arm circle and stride.

Later chapters will discuss how to adjust postures for individual movement pitches. For now, we discuss only the position of the fastball posture.

We mentioned earlier that the pitcher might bend forward during the windup. Whether slight or severe, the pitcher uses the bend to gain momentum into the pitch, therefore using it both functionally and stylistically. As posture pertains to the motion, we are strictly concerned with the position of posture once the arm circle begins its upward movement on the front side or as the stride leg begins its movement forward.

At this point (the start of the stride and the circle upward), regardless of the extent of the windup, the pitcher should set an upright posture. The spine should be nearly straight up, and the head should be directly over or slightly in front of the belly button. The pitcher should imagine staying as tall as possible throughout the motion.

At the landing and set of the stride foot, the head should be directly in the middle of the feet and over the center of the body. The pitcher maintains this position throughout the drive of the back leg. If posture is compromised, the location of the pitch will be affected.

Posture leaning to either side will affect side-to-side accuracy as well as balance. One thing to remember is that the body always follows the head. If the head sets off to the side, the body follows, and the tendency is for the ball to follow as well (see the sequence in figure 3.9). Because of the dominance

a   b

Figure 3.9 The head leaning to *(a)* the right or *(b)* the left will affect side-to-side accuracy, because the body follows the head and the ball usually follows the body.

of the arm circle, many pitchers lean the head toward the pitching-arm side, causing them to fall in that direction when finishing.

Likewise, posture positioning forward or backward will affect accuracy high and low. A popular move, especially for young pitchers, is bending the body forward. As previously mentioned, this is a subconscious effort to keep the ball from going too high. Indeed, bending forward at the waist will tend to keep the ball lower, but it will also cause the pitcher to go farther in the circle to release the ball in the strike zone. This additional movement will take her beyond her optimal position of power, reducing her speed. Leaning backward will tend to shoot the ball in an upward path (see figure 1.11 and 1.12 on page 15).

PRACTICE IT

A good drill to reinforce correct posture is for the pitcher to position herself on both knees at a 45-degree angle to the target (see figure 3.10). From the two-knees position, she pitches normally. If her head does not stabilize itself over her body, or if her spine bends in any direction, she will fall in that direction. As she continues to catch herself with her hands, the correction will sink in.

Correct posture is the key to balance. In fixing posture mistakes, however, corrections will often cause the pitcher to throw wild initially. Coaches should prepare the pitcher for this, create a positive environment, and ride out the control problems until the posture correction becomes a habit. Not only will control return, but it will also likely improve!

Figure 3.10 Pitch from a kneeling position with the knees at a 45-degree angle to the target.

CATCHING COMMON ERRORS

Let's take a look at some of the common mistakes made above the waist.

Jerky or interrupted arm circle. A misunderstanding of correct mechanics and a failure to understand the concept of natural movement usually causes this problem. The jerky arm circle usually leads to speed concerns and injuries. To correct this problem, the pitcher should start over with the basic drills. She should pay special attention to hand and ball positioning to start the circle and arm positioning throughout the circle. In addition, she should try glove-hand arm circles and keep all drill work close to a net and on one knee until progress occurs.

Arm circle behind back. This problem usually occurs because of a strength deficit somewhere in the upper body or arm. The body will attempt to compensate for the weakness. The problem is characterized by the arm taking an awkward path behind the pitcher's body and finishing at a severe angle outward from the pitcher's body. In other words, a right-handed pitcher with this problem would commonly pitch the ball into or behind a right-handed hitter. This problem can rarely be overcome without rehabilitation of the strength deficit. A sports medicine physician or physical therapist should be consulted.

Early load. An early load occurs when the pitcher turns the ball in a position to release before reaching the bottom of the circle. Normally, as the arm comes forward for a wrist snap at the bottom of the circle, the thumb automatically rotates toward the target and loads the ball for release (see figure 3.11a). This action allows the pitcher to gain fully from the whip down the back side of the circle.

Some pitchers, however, instinctively rotate the wrist (thumb downward) at the top of the circle or slightly below the top on the back side (see figure 3.11b). By doing so, they eliminate any opportunity to whip the ball through the back side. Instead of whipping the ball down the back side and past the hip, the pitcher essentially pushes the ball down the back side.

a   b

Figure 3.11   *(a)* The wrist rotates with the thumb toward the target at the bottom of the circle. *(b)* An early load with the wrist rotated closer to the top of the circle.

The pitcher who makes this mistake looks like she is giving all the energy and force she has, but the result does not match her efforts. She will struggle to develop speed. The correction is to keep the ball positioned outward or upward down the back side of the circle and allow the elbow to lead all the way to the body. Making this correction, unfortunately, is challenging because of the difficulty of feeling such a small movement during the aggressive arm circle.

PRACTICE IT   A visual aid that may help with this concept is holding a glass of water while going through the motion—slowly of course (see figure 3.12). Correct motion will allow the glass of water to stay upright until the bottom of the circle, approximately 12 to 18 inches behind the body when the arm begins to move forward for the wrist snap. At that point the water will spill out of the glass. Early loaders will spill the water as soon as they reach the back side of the circle up top.

Figure 3.12 Holding a glass of water while going slowly through the pitching motion.

PRACTICE IT

Another drill that can help the pitcher feel the movements uses a swimmer's noodle. The pitcher hangs her pitching arm straight down to the ground and grips the noodle (probably with some length cut off the end) so that the end of it solidly touches the ground. She starts the pitching circle. If she whips through the bottom of the zone, the noodle will not brush the ground. If the early load occurs, however, the end of the noodle will hit the ground (see figure 3.13).

PRACTICE IT

A drill that allows for a little faster arm movement while working on the correction of the early load is the football toss. The pitcher grips the football as if to throw a normal overhand pass. Using the

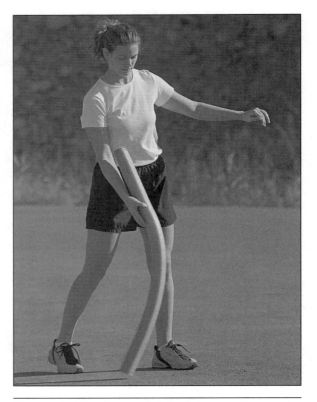

Figure 3.13 Correct whip of the noodle past the ground.

pitching motion, she makes the circle and releases the ball in front of her body. The point of the ball located closest to the pinky finger must be heading straight upward (see figure 3.14). The pitcher must not be afraid to throw the ball high with an arch. This would indicate that the elbow leads the circle. An early loader will release the football on a flat angle with the tip aiming outward left and right and the ball spinning forward. Another good aspect of this drill is the fact that it shows arm whip rather than straight-arm release. A pitcher who can get the point up in the air is leading correctly with the elbow. If the point goes directly outward to the

Figure 3.14 The point of the football should go upward instead of sideways or out toward the catcher.

catcher, the arm is straight. The pitcher should start this drill with a simple rock back and no circle, but she should eventually add the circle and distance to help strengthen the arm and reinforce proper mechanics.

Glove arm inactive or flying outward. The problem of the "dead" glove usually occurs simply because little or no thought has been given to the activity of the glove arm. The hand and arm fly outward usually due to a lack of functional strength and an inability to maintain the proper positioning.

PRACTICE IT

To ensure correct movement of the glove hand, the pitcher should try this simple drill. A catcher (or coach) stands in front of the pitcher about stride length plus two feet away. The catcher extends a glove or hand in front of herself about as high as the pitcher's stomach and over the power line. The pitcher should grip a washcloth or hand towel with her hands positioned about an inch apart (see figure 3.15a). She goes through the pitching circle naturally with both hands holding on to the washcloth until she reaches face or head level (see figure 3.15b). At that point, she lets go of the washcloth with the pitching hand and continues the arm circle to finish (see figure 3.15c). When the pitching hand lets go of the washcloth, the glove hand should pull the cloth downward, slapping the catcher's glove or hand at the finish (see figure 3.15d).

Figure 3.15 The towel drill: *(a)* Grip the towel with hands about an inch apart; *(b)* go through the circle with both hands; *(c)* at head level, let go of the towel with the pitching hand; and *(d)* slap the catcher's glove at the finish.

PRACTICE IT

Another drill for the glove hand has the pitcher leaving her glove on her hand. The coach should hold his or her glove or hand out in front of the pitcher about one to two feet in front of the pitcher's stride foot and over the power line. The pitcher should take the throwing hand and glove up the front side of the circle together. (The hand can be inside the glove or the two hands can just go separately but simultaneously.) When the throwing hand separates at face or head level and continues around the back side of the circle alone, the glove should drive down the front side of the circle and slap the coach's glove or hand out front (see figure 3.16). The arms will have moved in a jumping-jack motion on the way down.

Figure 3.16 The glove drives down the front of the circle and slaps the coach's glove.

Tight or restricted follow-through. This problem is characterized by the hand, forearm, elbow, or entire arm stopping at the body just as the ball is released. There is no dangling of the wrist and fingers. Instead, everything is stiff and rigid after (and sometimes during) the release of the ball. This problem is caused by a subconscious action by the pitcher to control the location of the ball.

PRACTICE IT

To fix this bad habit, the pitcher should try a simple tossing drill. She takes the ball and just lets the arm rock back a foot or so behind the hip. She rocks forward smoothly and tosses the ball to the catcher, who is standing (see figure 3.17). The pitcher should not be trying to throw a strike. She should simply toss the ball to the catcher. The catcher should gradually back up to full distance or perhaps a little farther. If the pitcher performs the toss correctly, she will be able to throw the distance with no problem. If the follow-through stiffens, the tosses will fall short or go sharply upward.

PRACTICE IT

The grab-the-net drill detailed earlier in this chapter is also an effective follow-through drill. Distance pitching will help, too, in maintaining a loose finish. Remember when working follow-throughs that the environment should always allow the pitcher to throw pitches that miss the target without causing damage. In other words, a pitch that misses the target simply hits a backstop or some type of net and drops to the floor or ground. Also keep in mind that the follow-through should happen as naturally as possible.

a

b

c

Figure 3.17 In the tossing drill, the pitcher rocks her arm back and then rocks forward and tosses to the catcher.

Posture leaning forward.   A lean forward is characterized by either a slight or severe bend at the waist that positions the head past the midpoint between the feet. The head often gets so far out front that it is over the front foot.

As mentioned in chapter 2, this problem can originate with a slow or nonexistent leg drive. The problem, like the tight follow-through, is also a subconscious attempt to control the ball from going too high. The two-knee drill, discussed earlier in this chapter, is excellent for helping the pitcher achieve proper balance.

PRACTICE IT   Another drill the pitcher can use to straighten up posture is to get positioned so that the stride foot will land about three feet in front of a wall or net. She starts with about 50 percent effort and throws the ball into the net or wall about head high or slightly above. (Use a Flexiball or rubber ball instead of a hard ball for this drill.) If posture is straight up and the pitcher does not miss the desired target low, the ball will ricochet off the wall or net and fly backward over her head (see figure 3.18). A catcher or coach can be positioned behind the pitcher to retrieve the balls. If the pitcher bends forward, she will be unable to perform this drill consistently with any success.

Figure 3.18   If the ball hits the wall at least head height, the ball will bounce back over the pitcher's head to the catcher standing behind the pitcher.

PRACTICE IT   One final posture drill to try when the pitcher is actually pitching a ball is the noodle drill. The coach takes a position to the glove-arm side of the pitcher and holds the foam swimmer's noodle about one foot behind where the pitcher's stride foot will contact the ground (see figure 3.19a). The noodle should stretch directly into the pitcher's path at the height of her face. The object of this drill is for the pitcher to pitch the ball without her face hitting the noodle (see figure 3.19b). The coach gradually backs up the noodle until the pitcher's head lands and holds the correct position. Pitches will likely be high and out of control until this positioning becomes more automatic.

a   b

Figure 3.19   In the noodle drill, (a) the coach holds the noodle, and (b) the pitcher goes through the pitching motion without touching the noodle.

Pitcher off balance toward the throwing-arm side.   Remember, where the head goes, the body and ball will follow. To put it in simpler terms, the ball goes where the nose goes! If the nose is up or back, the ball will tend to be high. If the nose is forward or down, the ball will tend to be low. With the nose right or left, the ball will tend to be right or left.

When a pitcher is off balance, centering the head before reaching the contact point of the stride leg will usually solve the problem. Off-balance pitching will adversely affect control and speed. If a pitcher is specifically off balance to the throwing-arm side, she should pitch half speed through the entire motion and freeze with all her body weight on one leg (the stride leg) after release for about five seconds (see figure 3.20). Off-balance pitchers usually cannot balance on the stride leg but instead must quickly catch themselves with the drive leg.

By initially backing off speed, the pitcher should be able to concentrate on head positioning. But if she cannot gain balance on her own, she should use some sort of physical block so that her body cannot fall in the direction of her tendency (see figure 3.21). This block should be something that would be a deterrent but not dangerous if she repeats the mistake.

Figure 3.20 Here the pitcher freezes with all her weight on the stride leg after release.

Figure 3.21 A physical block, such as a bag, can be placed to help the pitcher avoid falling to the side.

One of my favorite tools is the pitcher's balance beam. The balance beam should be solidly constructed of wood or metal, at least eight inches wide and eight feet long (see figure 3.22a). The beam does not need be extremely high off the ground—three to five inches is sufficient. Tape or paint should mark a power line down the middle.

The pitcher should start at low speed to become comfortable on the beam. She must remember to stay in the middle of the beam with her stride on the power line (see figure 3.22b). The balance beam is a great tool to help pitchers concentrate on their power-line step and their balance.

a   b

Figure 3.22   *(a)* A balance beam can be built like this one; *(b)* the pitcher using the beam to practice balance and staying on the power line.

THE FINAL PITCH

The pitcher must be particular and precise with overall mechanics while still allowing natural motion within the arm circle itself. One of the biggest mistakes pitchers make in working on correct mechanics is focusing on the location of the pitch. Eventually, focus points and foot placements will be used to work on locations, but while working on the fundamentals, coaches should get off the buckets and put the targets away.

When a pitcher is attempting to change a bad habit, the catcher should stand up to catch or better yet, the pitcher should just throw openly into a net. Wrist snap will be a big asset to upper-body action and will increase the speed of the ball. Although there are hundreds of wrist-snap exercises, none will be effective if the pitcher stifles the follow-through. All drills should reinforce the mechanics that the pitcher hopes to imprint into the memory banks of her muscles.

TIMING OF THE MOTION

4

After having examined the mechanics of the upper and lower body separately, it is time to look at how they work together. The pitching motion can accurately be described as aggressive, even violent. But in its truest form it is also a harmony of movement—a combination of power, speed, balance, and finesse that can appear almost effortless.

GETTING THE BODY TO WORK AS A WHOLE

Ultimately, the goal is to get the entire body to work as one unit. To obtain this objective while pitching the softball, the timing of the movements throughout the motion will be crucial. Having a solid base of upper- and lower-body mechanics is a big advantage in working on timing. If the pitcher does not understand the power line, for example, she will bring many upper- and lower-body mistakes into the equation, muddying the water considerably from the start.

In a nutshell, the pitcher must remember the rules: the front side strides forward and the back side drives through. When we first work with a pitcher, we videotape her from the pitching-arm side to see the particulars of the timing. We place the camera directly to the side and as close to the pitcher as possible while allowing all body movements, including the stride and top of the arm circle, to remain viewable (see figure 4.1). Seeing the path of the ball is not necessary. The objective is to produce a videotape of the pitching motion that we can replay in slow motion and see exactly what is happening and when.

To create a common terminology, we relate all movements to the face of a clock. As we look at the videotape and the pitcher from the side, we imagine a clock over the body with the center of the clock located on the pitcher's chest. That will put twelve o'clock directly over her head, three o'clock (for a right-handed pitcher) directly out in front of the chest, six o'clock straight down to the ground, and nine o'clock (for a right-handed pitcher) directly out on the back side of the circle. (Three o'clock and nine o'clock would be opposite for a left-handed pitcher.) See figure 4.2.

Figure 4.1 This is the view you should have through the video camera.

Figure 4.2 Use the clock face as a guide to arm position.

SETTING THE STRIDE FOOT

All the body placements will be measured once the stride foot has been set. The set position of the stride foot means that the foot will be flat, weight will be toward the ball of the foot, and the foot will be prepared to accept the weight shift of the back side. If just the heel or toe of the stride foot is contacting the ground, the foot is not yet set.

Remember that when using proper mechanics the pitcher strides aggressively and lands on a flat foot with her weight mostly on the ball of the foot. Once the foot is set, take a good look at the following areas: drive foot, posture, pitching-arm appearance, pitching-arm location, and glove hand.

Drive Foot

At the set of the stride foot, the drive foot should be rolled up on the tiptoe and holding no weight. The knee of the drive leg should be directed toward the catcher. The knee need not be aimed perfectly at the catcher, but it should be pointed in that general direction. The knee should definitely not be pointing toward the camera.

If the knee is not directed toward the catcher, we can predict an inefficient back side even at this early point in the motion analysis. As mentioned earlier, there simply is not enough time to rotate the hips and knee totally to 90 degrees of the target and recover before the release of the ball.

Posture

At the set of the stride foot, the posture of the back should be straight up with the head centered in the middle of the stride between the feet. In relation to the imaginary clock, the head should be located directly toward twelve o'clock.

Pitching-Arm Appearance

At the set of the stride foot, notice the appearance of the pitching arm. If correct, it should resemble a banana rather than a straight line. If the curve or looseness is absent at the set of the stride foot, keep an eye on the arm to see when, if ever, it falls into the whipping position. This observation reveals whether the pitcher is using the entire circle for speed, half the circle, a quarter of the circle, or whatever. Also, if the arm is straight, notice the point at which it straightens. Is it in the windup or at the beginning of the circle?

Pitching-Arm Location

The most important piece of the timing puzzle is the location of the pitching arm. At the set position of the stride foot, the pitching hand and ball should be located somewhere between twelve o'clock and ten o'clock for a right-handed pitcher (between twelve o'clock and two o'clock for a left-handed pitcher). This positioning of the arm is crucial because it will determine how much time and opportunity the pitcher has to drive the back side into the pitch.

In other words, if the stride foot is set while the ball is at the top of the circle (between twelve o'clock and ten o'clock for a right-handed pitcher), then the pitcher has about half the circle left to drive the back side through. The lower the ball gets before the stride foot is set, the shorter the time available to drive the body through. If the pitcher doesn't set the stride foot until the ball is at eight o'clock or seven o'clock, even if she understands the mission of driving the back side through, she will not have enough time to do so before she releases the ball.

Many questions surround the exact location of the drive leg at release. The key to effective use of the drive leg is to move it forward immediately after setting the stride foot. The pitcher should move the drive leg as aggressively as possible in conjunction with the throwing arm. Correct functioning of the drive leg will deliver the back side of the body smoothly into the front side. If the drive leg moves slowly, posture will be forward and the rear of the pitcher will stick out toward the side or back.

Glove Hand

At the set of the stride foot, in relation to the imaginary clock, the glove hand should be positioned at least as high as three o'clock (nine o'clock for a left-hander) and could go as high as one o'clock (eleven o'clock for a left-hander).

The arms should be in sync when the pitching arm comes down the back side of the circle.

CATCHING COMMON ERRORS

Pitchers with sound mechanics will usually have reasonably accurate timing. When problems occur, such as the arm circle being too low when the foot is set, we must check the elements of the stride. Pitchers often land heel to toe. Looking at a few pitchers in slow motion will reveal the consequence of this landing. Pitchers have made thousands of forward strides since they began walking, all of them with a heel-to-toe landing. The pitcher must differentiate pitching from walking and understand the distinctive nature of the stride-foot landing.

If the landing of the foot is not a problem, the next point to check is the height of the stride leg. If the knee goes to a parallel or nearly parallel point with the hip and the foot is landing too late, the pitcher can simply lower the stride. (If the timing is OK, she can leave the stride alone.) Remember that it is not necessary or desirable to shorten the stride. The pitcher can lower the stride slightly and still reach the same length.

In looking at timing, we will be able to see the rippling effects of fundamental mistakes. Mistakes made above the waist can have negative effects below the waist and vice versa. Borrowing from the adage that one bad apple can spoil the whole bunch, we might say that one bad mechanic can spoil the whole delivery.

PRACTICE IT

One of my favorite drills for timing is the towel drill. This drill is also an excellent way for a pitcher to practice without having to have a real catcher or a place to throw. (I stole this drill from Tom House and Nolan Ryan and turned it around to fit our fastpitch needs!)

The towel drill requires a regular hand towel. The pitcher should get an inexpensive one and keep it in her bag. The towel will come in handy for warming up as well as practicing. The pitcher should grip the towel with three or four fingers on one side and the thumb opposite the fingers on the other side (see figure 4.3). A partner or catcher should stand in front of the pitcher about two feet ahead of where the stride foot lands. The partner should face the pitcher and hold a hand or glove out in front, directly over the power line. The pitcher should go

Figure 4.3   The grip of the towel for the towel drill.

a

b

Figure 4.4 The towel drill motion: *(a)* the towel at the top of the circle and *(b)* after slapping the partner's hand.

through her regular motion and slap the towel through the partner's hand (see figure 4.4a and b). The partner can tell the pitcher whether the towel hit squarely or hit off the edge of the thumb or pinky. A hit off the edge would indicate a pitch that would not have been located down the power line and over the plate.

The pitcher should do the towel drills in sets of 10, repeating as many times as possible in a night. She might want to do a set of 10 every time a commercial comes on during an hour of watching television. Because the towel drill does not require much space, performing it is easy. The drill should be done at full speed. The towel drill will help the pitcher with several aspects of the motion:

- **Setting posture.** If posture is off in any direction, the pitcher will struggle to hit the hand. If her posture is forward, she will probably be falling into the partner.
- **Power line.** By freezing at the end of the towel slap, the pitcher can check to see whether the stride foot is on the power line. As mentioned earlier, the drill is also a great way to check the power-line pull of the pitching hand.
- **Wrist snap.** The slapping of the towel on the hand or glove encourages an aggressive wrist snap, especially if the hand happens to be attached to a brother or sister!
- **Back-leg drive.** If the back leg hangs back or delays, the pitcher will most likely fall short of reaching the hand.
- **Follow-through.** To gain a good slap of the towel against the hand or glove, the pitcher must follow through with the wrist snap. In addition, because the hand or glove is located out in front of the pitcher, if the elbow stops at the side the towel will never reach its destination.

Both the partner and the pitcher should make sure that the pitcher uses proper mechanics throughout the towel drill.

In working on specific timing problems, the pitcher should be familiar with the easy-to-do shadow drills. The shadow drills let the pitcher be in full motion but without the ball, allowing her to focus on a specific area that she needs to improve. Many of the below-the-waist drills can be used to work on overall body motion as well.

THE FINAL PITCH

The synchronizing of movement is essential in nearly every sport. Ice-skating, golf, basketball, tennis, swimming, lacrosse, rowing, gymnastics, and volleyball all require the athlete to time body movement to be effective. Fastpitch softball pitching is no exception.

The key to timing in pitching is setting the front foot quickly. The other elements of mechanics rely heavily on the initial stride-leg fundamental. In learning the fundamentals, the pitcher need not concern herself with the timing aspect until she has a grasp of the basic movements. The timing aspect will often take care of itself. This timing element will be the single biggest contributor to the efficiency of the fastpitch motion.

At this point the pitcher can also begin to realize the level of precision required to get things right. Parents as well as pitchers often question the significance of details such as whether the stride lands on the heel of the foot or the sole of the foot. After pitchers see the videotape, understand the concept, and realize that a heel-toe landing can cost a pitcher up to three clock-face numbers in relationship to timing, the emphasis on the particulars seems justified.

CONSISTENCY, LOCATION, AND SPEED

5

Among the most popular questions of fastpitch is whether the pitcher should initially stress speed or accuracy. The answer is a resounding *neither*. What the pitcher should focus on first is the topic of the previous four chapters—fundamental mechanics.

As far as speed goes, the pitcher should be using maximum effort. This is the formula:

$$\text{consistent speed} + \text{consistent mechanics} = \text{consistent location}$$

The only way a pitcher can produce consistent speed is to use total effort. It would be impossible, for example, to pitch consistently at 85 percent of total effort. Some pitches might be at 78 percent, others at 87 percent. Each speed would require a distinct release point to generate the same result. If speed were the same, however, the release point would be the same.

With consistency in mechanics and speed, the pitcher will be able to make simple adjustments and gain pinpoint accuracy through practice. On the other hand, if the pitcher's body mechanics are different with every pitch or the speed tends to vary with each pitch, control and pinpoint accuracy will be elusive for the pitcher.

Think about the particularities of free-throw shooters or dart throwers. When good players shoot free throws or throw darts, they try to be sure that on every attempt the feet, hand, and body are in exactly the same spot. Imagine a free-throw shooter shooting one free throw from a set position, the next with a jump shot, the next with a hook shot, and finally an attempt with a granny shot. How would the shooter ever make an adjustment? The same principle applies to pitching; if the pitcher knows where everything is and has a concept of timing the speed of release, she can easily make slight adjustments to change the location of the pitch.

The pitcher must beware of overemphasizing control before she achieves good mastery of the basics. Almost everyone who has ever spent time at a ballfield has heard the famous coaching advice, "Just slow it down and throw strikes!" Although this advice is well intended, it can lead to the pitcher's demise.

A pitcher who grows up and gains experience that is prioritized by "just throwing strikes" will be a pitcher who will always struggle to cut loose and never come close to her speed potential. Anyone who has ever developed and matured as a pitcher, even the greatest, will tell stories of pitches and games in which they were out of control.

During the learning process, periods when growth occurs will often be accompanied by a loss of accuracy. But if the pitcher sticks to the goal of pitching with consistent speed and consistent mechanics, she will soon regain accuracy and will have progressed to another level. The pitcher who grows up "just throwing strikes" will someday be 17 years old with a 50-mile-per-hour fastball lurking fat in the strike zone. And she will be pitching just as she has been instructed for her entire career.

Such pitchers often hesitate to break out of the control mode and take risks with new pitches or speed advancement because loss of control devastates them. Loss of control, however, is usually a by-product of progress.

If a pitcher cannot throw enough strikes at full speed to compete in a game, then she is not ready to pitch in a game. It's that simple. Note that throwing enough strikes to compete does not mean throwing all strikes or striking out every batter. It simply means that the pitcher can throw enough strikes to hitters to avoid walking five or six batters in a row. Until the pitcher reaches that point, she must practice until her strike-ball ratio favors strikes. Then she has earned another try. This method is a much better option than compromising one of the major attributes of the position.

HIGHS AND LOWS

In learning control and location of the pitch, the pitcher should keep things simple. The first thing to establish is a straight-ahead, down-the-middle, power-line pitch. This pitch goes right along with the basic lineup of the feet. The pitching arm simply follows the established line.

Once the pitcher starts to get consistent with the power line, she should move on to height. The common correction for a pitch that goes too high is to tell the pitcher that she held the ball too long. With the pitch that goes too low, the opposite applies. The rationale is that the pitcher let go too soon. To fix control, most fans, parents, and coaches call out a logical correction to the pitcher: "Hold on a little longer," or "Let go a little sooner."

As sensible as that adjustment may sound, think about the practicality of it. The entire arm circle starts and finishes in less than a second. Is it feasible that anyone, especially a beginner, could make the tiny adjustment that would be necessary to follow that theory? Usually, pitchers nod and seem to understand, but the correction results are slow in coming.

For that reason, consider an easier approach. First, the pitcher must establish a *focus point*. The focus point should be very small. A catchy slogan for the pitcher is to make the focus point "as big as a bug." Note that the glove is *not* always the focus point. The focus point might be a tiny part of the glove, but it would not be the entire glove.

Pitchers should learn to establish focus points as they begin their warm-ups with overhand throwing. Many athletes have difficulty locking on to a particular spot and maintaining that lock until delivery of a throw or pitch.

Pitchers will have to practice this technique to become comfortable and consistent. Once they master it, however, they will be surprised at how much this simple technique will help them locate their pitches.

To start to work on height adjustment, the pitcher should pick a focus point on the intended target itself. After a couple of pitches, if the location is too high or too low the pitcher simply moves the focus point to adjust.

For instance, if the target is knee high, the catcher places the glove at knee height. The pitcher establishes the focus point somewhere on the glove. If after a couple of pitches it is obvious that the pitcher is missing the target too high, she should move her focus point to something underneath the intended target. For example, she can make the focus point the catcher's shoe or maybe even the plate or the ground. The pitcher should attempt to pitch the ball to the focus point. The pitcher must realize that the focus point location does not matter as long as she gains the correct result. If she is looking at the catcher's foot and throwing knee-high strikes, that's great! Figure 5.1 shows how to change the focus point.

To wrap it all up in a neat little package for you, the pitcher should not make technical adjustments with body positioning to control the height of the pitch. *She simply moves her eyes up or down and adjusts the focus point.*

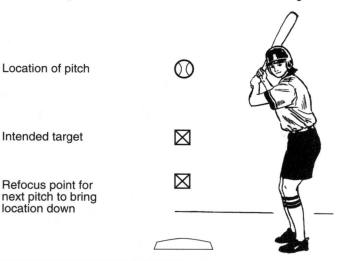

Location of pitch

Intended target

Refocus point for next pitch to bring location down

Figure 5.1 Changing the focus point to improve accuracy.

The bonus to this method occurs when the pitcher finds it difficult to concentrate, perhaps when the game is tense. Instead of hearing a plea from the coach to concentrate, a request often hard for her to implement, she will hear the suggestion to focus. The pitcher will immediately translate this idea to the task of finding her "bug" and locking on to it until release. Carrying out that mission will automatically trigger concentration! Bingo!

INSIDE AND OUTSIDE

The pitcher can use two options for controlling the path of the ball from side to side. The first, steering with the hand, is the one that most pitchers automatically adopt. Remember, though, that we are trying to gain precision. With the finger placement on the ball and the aggressive arm action, this steering method will often prove difficult to master, especially with adequate consistency. Some pitchers will master the technique and be fine until they hit the movement pitches. Then, in using the method of steering with the hand, they lose some effectiveness of the movement.

In learning fundamentals, the goal is to establish foundations on which to build. The pitcher should try to avoid going backward. For that reason, to attain the highest level of accuracy and make a smooth transition into the movement pitches, the pitcher should use the second option for side-to-side control—steering the ball with the stride foot.

Remember from the fundamentals that the foot (drive foot), toe (stride foot), and target line up in the footwork. The pitcher maintains that alignment no matter where the target is located. She imagines a straight line from the drive foot through the target when she takes her stance on the rubber. The toe of the stride foot lands directly on the imaginary line, maintaining the 45-degree angle. The drive-leg knee drives down the line (drive toe to stride heel), and the hand follows down the line as usual. Essentially, the power line is established to the target, whatever that target may be (see figure 5.2).

Figure 5.2 The feet lined up to throw (a) outside and (b) inside the power line.

This procedure allows all the action above the waist (wrist snap, follow-through, shoulders, posture, etc.) to perform the necessary movements for the pitch, as always. A smooth transition from steering the fastball to steering the rise or drop is therefore in place. If mechanics are solid before the pitcher tries this, she will see immediate positive results.

In addition, the impact proper mechanics have on a pitcher's ability to improve to the next level will become obvious. If the pitcher has not first established a consistent power line, how can she possibly make adjustments for side-to-side control?

TARGET LOCATIONS

In learning to throw to targets, the pitcher can practice with two basic sets of targets. The first set allows the pitcher to throw to one location at a time. Refer to the face of a clock over the strike zone. The four targets are twelve o'clock, three o'clock, six o'clock, and nine o'clock, as shown in figure 5.3. Twelve o'clock is located over the middle of the plate chest high, six o'clock is over the middle and knee high, three o'clock is in the middle heightwise but on the inside corner, and nine o'clock is in the middle heightwise but on the outside corner.

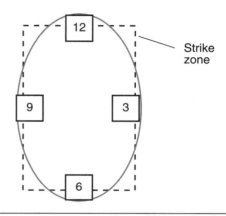

Figure 5.3 Targets at twelve o'clock, three o'clock, six o'clock, and nine o'clock in relation to the strike zone.

For twelve o'clock and six o'clock, the pitcher steps on a straight-ahead power line and focuses either high or low to hit the target. For three o'clock and nine o'clock, the pitcher must step slightly left or right to get the ball inside or outside, maintaining the height of the pitch down the middle. These targets are a simple version because they require using only one fine point at a time (either high, low, in, or out).

The other set of targets are located at one o'clock, five o'clock, seven o'clock, and eleven o'clock, as shown in figure 5.4. These targets require precision in two directions and move the locations

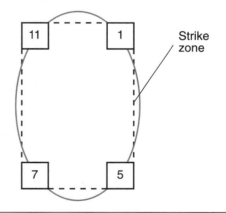

Figure 5.4 Targets at one o'clock, five o'clock, seven o'clock, and eleven o'clock in relation to the strike zone.

to the four corners of the zone, toward the probable weaknesses of the hitter. For one o'clock and five o'clock, the pitcher must step toward the inside of the plate and focus either high or low according to the target. For seven o'clock and eleven o'clock, the pitcher must step toward the outside of the plate and focus either high or low according to the target.

COLORS OF THE STRIKE ZONE

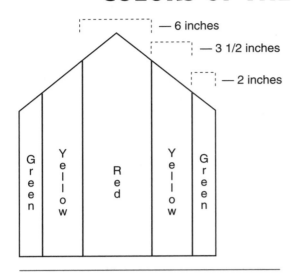

Figure 5.5 The three colors of the strike zone.

Now let's get a little more detailed with zone locations. To make understanding easier and create a simple terminology that pitchers, catchers, and coaches can use to communicate, imagine the zone striped in three colors (see figure 5.5).

Red is the color of the zone located in the middle. Heightwise, red is from the top of the legs to the top of the stomach on the hitter. Widthwise, red is about the middle six inches of the plate.

Yellow is the color of the zone located toward the edges but not *on* the edges. Heightwise, yellow is above the stomach but not quite to the armpit and slightly above the knee to the top of the leg. Widthwise, yellow is away from the middle and toward the edge of the plate but not quite to the corner.

Green is the color of the zone located on the edges. Heightwise, green is from the chest on up and from the knees on down. Widthwise, green is from the corners or edges of the plate on out. Notice that I used the terms *on up, on down,* and *on out* to describe the location of the green zone. This is because it goes as far as the batters will swing or as far as the umpire will call the strike.

Now in pitching, we have a few guidelines:

- We want to get ahead and stay ahead of the hitter.
- The hitter has two choices.
- We must play the odds with called strikes and balls.

First, we want to get ahead and stay ahead of the hitter. This simply refers to the pitcher's having more strikes than balls in the count. The count affects both the pressure factor and pitch selection. If the pitcher is ahead in the count, the pressure is on the hitter. If the hitter is ahead in the count, the pressure is on the pitcher. If the pitcher is ahead in the count, she can throw pitches she prefers to throw. When behind in the count, she must throw pitches the hitter would like to hit. A pitcher who pitches ahead in the count will typically have a higher number of strikeouts and a greater degree of success than a pitcher who pitches behind in the count.

The hitter has two choices: swing or take. She can do either at any time. By observing hitters over time, we may notice tendencies such as a certain hitter or a certain team always taking a first strike; swinging at a first strike; fishing for high, low, inside, or outside pitches; looking at third strikes; and so forth.

In playing the odds with strikes and balls, the pitcher must understand several truths:

- The hitter has two choices.
- Red-zone pitches will *almost always* be a called strike from the umpire. Red-zone pitches are pitches that the hitter has the best chance of hitting

solidly. For this reason, if the pitcher needs a strike to be called, red is her best bet, if she is willing to pay the consequences if the hitter decides to swing. Red-zone pitches are the pitches hitters most want to hit. See figure 5.6 for the percentages for each zone.

- Yellow-zone pitches will *probably* be a called strike by the umpire. Hitters have less chance of making contact with a yellow-zone pitch and hitting it solidly. For this reason, yellow pitches are excellent pitches to throw to get ahead of the batter. The pitcher plays decent odds both ways— whether the hitter swings or takes.

- Green-zone pitches *might or might not* be a called strike from the umpire. Green-zone pitches offer the lowest probability for the hitter to make contact and succeed. For this reason, green pitches are the pitches that pitchers most want to pitch.

Having understood all the facts, the pitcher must be smart when locating pitches. She should play the odds. In other words, she should not throw a green pitch to open the count, then whine and gripe when the hitter takes the pitch and the umpire calls it a ball. The hitter can be choosy with no count and can take a pitch on the edge of the zone. The pitcher knew from the start that the umpire might or might not call the pitch a strike. Even though it may have been a beautiful pitch, it was the wrong pitch for the situation.

Many coaches tell pitchers to always throw a ball with an 0-2 or 1-2 count. This is incorrect. With an 0-2 or 1-2 count, the pitch should be in the green zone. If the pitcher wants the hitter to swing, she must offer a pitch that will tempt the hitter. An obvious ball will entice only a poor hitter. If the hitter does not follow the rule to "swing if it's close," the umpire *might* ring her up. If the umpire doesn't, nothing is lost. What would be the point of getting ahead if the pitcher is just going to throw automatic balls until the count is

Red	**If the hitter takes . . .** *High* chance that umpire will call the pitch a strike. **If the hitter swings . . .** *High* chance the hitter will make solid contact with the ball.
Yellow	**If the hitter takes . . .** The umpire will *probably* call a strike. **If the hitter swings . . .** The location of the ball is in a lower percentage area for the hitter to make solid contact with the ball.
Green	**If the hitter takes . . .** The umpire might or might not call a strike. **If the hitter swings . . .** The location of the ball is in the lowest percentage area for the hitter to succeed in making contact and/or making solid contact.

Figure 5.6 Percentages of success for hitters in the three zones.

even again? The point of getting ahead is to throw the strikeout pitch. Strikeout pitches are green!

Although the rulebook designates the strike zone, most of us realize that no two umpires establish exactly the same zone. Therefore, the umpire will dictate what is yellow and what is green. The pitcher should discover this early in the game and work accordingly. She should not constantly fight the established zone. She should base her strategies on what she knows to be the facts and percentages regarding the zones. Gambling on exceptions is a losing proposition.

In this chapter, we discuss targets as they pertain to fastballs. The complexity of the colors of the zone, however, applies to all pitches, as we will discuss further in part II.

IMPROVING ACCURACY

The pitcher should use checkpoints throughout the warm-up process. These checkpoints are the fundamentals such as a loose follow-through, power line, balance, posture, back-leg drive, and so on. Initially, when the pitcher begins the underhand motion, she should just toss to the catcher, who should remain standing. Too often pitchers will toss overhand but immediately lock up and try to go all out when they start throwing underhand.

The pitcher should instead toss and gradually work up to the faster speeds. This method encourages a loose approach to the motion. From the beginning and throughout the warm-up, the pitcher should be conscious of the checkpoints, considering one point at a time to be sure that everything is in place.

The pitcher should not immediately emphasize control. The catcher should stand through the first half of the warm-up. When the checkpoints seem consistently correct, the pitcher can change the power line to the left and right. Pitching to each side of the catcher's body is a good way to do this. Checkpoints must remain intact (especially balance) during the power-line adjustment. This can all be done in warm-ups to ensure that proper mechanics are in place for the game.

PRACTICE IT

Most pitchers seem to find the high targets naturally. Usually, the low pitch causes most of the problems in accuracy, posture adjustment, follow-through, and so on. A great drill to learn lower release points is the one-skip drill. To do the one-skip drill, the pitcher should choose a focus point about five feet in front of the plate (see figure 5.7). The object is to one skip the ball to the catcher without adjusting or compromising form. If the ball is higher than the target, the pitcher should change the focus point to a lower spot. After the pitcher masters the one skip, she can try throwing to a glove placed as a target at the ground behind the plate. Focusing on one small spot, the pitcher throws into the glove or short hops the ball in front of the glove, changing focus if necessary. For fun, she can throw into a five-gallon bucket with the open end toward her, as shown in figure 5.8. Sometimes, if she hits the bucket just right, it will stand up! Notice how many of these pitches end up knee high, making the point that from down low it is usually helpful to focus slightly lower than

Figure 5.7 Positioning for the one-skip drill.

Figure 5.8 Throwing to a bucket.

the target. To end the drill, the pitcher can finish with some knee-high pitches. She must be careful, though, not to raise her focus point too high.

PRACTICE IT   By performing the one-skip drill against a concrete wall, the pitcher can hit the ground directly in front of the wall, skip the ball into the wall, and have the ball return to her in the air (see figure 5.9). This is an excellent way for the pitcher to work alone, but she must remember to stay true to her form.

PRACTICE IT   In working side to side, the pitcher can work alone and become accustomed to various step locations by standing in the middle of a room. Someone can call out different objects in the room—the corner of the coffee table, the lamp, the coat rack, the glass of water, the plant, the left side of the television—and the pitcher can stride toward the object and finish through the pitch. This drill, of course, is done without the ball.

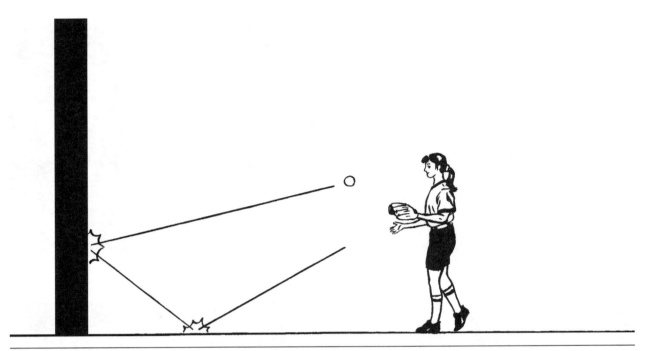

Figure 5.9 The path of the ball in the one-skip drill against a wall.

PRACTICE IT Another way to practice side to side is to work on the balance beam. With the beam turned slightly to indicate inside or outside, the pitcher can feel what it is like to step directly to the target (see figure 5.10). This drill is also beneficial for pitchers who are learning the proper power-line step when using a movement pitch. The balance beam forces the foot to go in the right direction, and the pitcher can focus on completing the correct mechanics.

PRACTICE IT Side-to-side practice added to the towel drill will help the pitcher gain muscle memory and increase repetitions to the locations. The catcher or helper in the towel drill, instead of holding the hand directly in front of the pitcher as mentioned in chapter 4, can hold both hands out

Figure 5.10 Turn the balance beam slightly so that the pitcher can practice stepping directly to the target.

slightly to the left and right of center (see figure 5.11). The pitcher alternately steps back and forth to each hand while slapping it with the towel.

Pitchers, catchers, and coaches often believe that a pitcher is more accurate at pitching to targets than she actually is. This conclusion comes from random tracking of accuracy and allowing many pitches to count because they were "close enough." Remember that the plate is only 17 inches wide. A slight miss can easily mean the difference in zone color from green to yellow or yellow to red. Charting is a good method of tracking accuracy.

To chart a pitcher's accuracy, use stationary targets taped to a wall or hung on a net. The targets should be no larger than six-inch-by-six-inch squares (see figure 5.12). The targets should be placed at twelve o'clock, three o'clock, six o'clock, and nine o'clock or at one o'clock, five o'clock, seven o'clock, and eleven o'clock. The pitcher pitches 10 times to each target. The 10 pitches can be consecutive or mixed, but a hit or miss should be recorded for each pitch. If the pitcher hits 4 of 10, she is 40 percent accurate on that target.

The pitcher can work toward percentage goals. The catcher and whoever else may be calling pitches should know the current percentages because that information will help them decide what pitch to call in a given situation.

Figure 5.11 In a variation of the towel drill, the catcher holds both hands out, and the pitcher alternately slaps both hands.

Figure 5.12 Stationary targets taped to a wall.

IMPROVING SPEED AND POWER

Because the name of the game is to pitch fast, this topic is of interest to most pitchers, parents, and coaches. But be careful not to be ridiculous when it comes to speed. The pitcher and others must be realistic in what they attempt. I have some daddies who want to know why their 65-pound, 10-year-old daughter is not throwing as hard as the 95-pound 11-year-old. The pitcher should take notice of several factors when working on or wishing for speed increases.

• Effort is, more often than not, legitimately lacking. Girls seem to seek perfection more than they do speed, and many do not put their maximum effort into each pitch. Take a look at the pitcher. Does pitching make her fatigued? If not, drills will be more helpful than just repeating "Throw harder" every pitch.

• Natural physical characteristics cannot be changed. Body type and genetics will yield natural strengths such as longer levers, more developed muscles, fast-twitch muscle capability, and so on. Every player can improve her strength, but she should not expect the impossible. A five-foot-five-inch basketball player is not going to dunk the ball.

• Length of stride can be worked on and improved. The pitcher must have sound mechanics and must not overdo stride length. She should still be able to drive the back leg into the pitch. The more aggressive the legs and stride are, the more aggressive the entire body will be. Also, remember that the closer the pitcher gets to the hitter, the faster she appears.

• Quickness of the stride foot can also be improved. The body has an innate sense of the timing involved in pitching. The arm is trying to be at a certain point by the time the stride foot lands. If the speed of the stride foot increases, the arm will likely increase to keep the timing in sync.

• Particular mechanics can usually be improved even after they are mastered. Videotape should be checked at least twice a year to be sure that the pitcher maintains the following speed mechanics: loose wrist snap, smooth natural arm circle, loose follow-through, correct posture, and good balance.

Several drills are effective in working on the previously mentioned improvable factors.

PRACTICE IT

Triple and Double Circles

The pitcher kneels on one knee close to a net or fence (right knee down for a right-handed pitcher). She makes her arm circle three times in a row as fast as she can before releasing the ball and tries to become faster with each circle. She should use muscles throughout the arm to make the circles, not just spin at the shoulder. (A slight curve to the arm rather than a straight arm indicates involvement of the whole arm.) The pitcher performs 10 pitches, then drops to double circles for 10 pitches. She finishes with single circles but puts all the energy of the multiple circles into the single circle.

PRACTICE IT ## Stride Drills

Stride aggression can be improved in several ways. The coach can observe the pitcher's stride on several pitches without her realizing that the coach is trying to get an honest idea of her natural stride. The coach then places a chalk mark where her toe is landing and another three or four inches in front of the first. The pitcher should try to reach the new mark. If that is easy, the distance can be increased by another three or four inches. The pitcher should not attempt to do too much at one time.

Knowing the natural stride of the pitcher, the coach can place a rope in front of her at about three-quarters the full distance of her stride. The rope can be four to five inches off the ground. This placement will encourage the pitcher to stride out farther as well as drive the stride leg (by forcing it to stay higher longer). The distance and height of the rope can be changed reasonably and gradually. But the pitcher must keep in mind the timing that must occur with the stride-foot landing and the arm between ten o'clock and twelve o'clock (see figure 5.13).

Figure 5.13 The pitcher strides over the rope, working on extension of the stride length.

PRACTICE IT ## Speed Drills

Speed drills are exactly what the name implies. The catcher is an important part of this drill. The pitcher should take her place on the mound. After someone says, "Go," the pitcher begins to pitch a predetermined number of pitches, pitching the ball as fast and as quickly as she can. She drives her back leg through normally and stays in tune with other correct mechanics. As soon as she finishes a pitch, she hurries back to the rubber and sets her feet for the next pitch. Meanwhile, the catcher catches the ball and throws it back as fast as she can. The pitcher should be on the rubber to catch the throw and immediately pitch again. She omits the windup and makes just the circle before release. The scale that follows is a good guide for timing a series of pitches. It is helpful to use two balls. The pitcher starts with one, and the catcher with another. The catcher, who should be standing, should not throw her ball until she has caught the pitch.

Number of pitches	Minimum time in seconds
10	30
12	36
15	45
20	60

During the year the pitcher should build up to a speed-drill workout of 60 pitches, which could be six sets of 10, five sets of 12, four sets of 15, or three sets of 20. She should do the sets at the end of a normal workout.

PRACTICE IT

Overweighting and Underweighting

The use of heavy and light balls has proved to be extremely effective in increasing speed. The best program I have found is an eight-week program that requires a pitcher to do a certain workout three times per week. The ball weight should be kept within a reasonable range. Most biomechanists recommend that the ball be no more than 20 percent over or under the standard softball weight, which would be approximately 1.25 ounces if using the standard weight of a 12-inch ball ($6\frac{1}{4}$ to $6\frac{1}{2}$ ounces). With extensive testing, I have found a 1- to 2-ounce difference to work quite well with established pitchers. See figure 5.14 for an 8-week weighted-ball workout program developed by Club K. The key to over- and underweighting, however, is balancing the two. The heavier ball will build strength, and the lighter ball will put speed on that strength. Using both balls balances the equation. If the pitcher overdoes the weights one way or the other, she will compromise mechanics and learn bad habits. Even worse, she may injure herself.

PRACTICE IT

Harness Training

Ankle harnesses can be used to increase strength in the legs (when resisted) or create quicker leg drive (when assisted). A piece of theratubing attached to an ankle harness balances the forces. The pitcher should perform an assisted leg drive for 10 pitches and then a resisted leg drive for 10 pitches. For the resisted leg drive, the ankle harness goes around the ankle of the drive leg. A coach or partner should take a position behind the pitcher. The theratubing should be extended but not pulled (see figure 5.15a), and there should be no slack in the tubing. The pitcher should stride forward and drive the back leg as normally as possible. The resistance can be adjusted but not to the extent that it changes the pitcher's mechanics or inhibits the drive pattern. The pitcher can actually pitch into a net or fence on the resisted drill. For the assisted leg drive, the coach

Week 1		Week 2		Week 3		Week 4	
75%-80% speed	Warm up 50 times with standard ball	75%-80% speed	Warm up 50 times with standard ball	75%-80% speed	Warm up 50 times with standard ball	75%-80% speed	Warm up 50 times with standard ball
100% speed	9 times with standard ball	100% speed	9 times with standard ball	100% speed	10 times with standard ball	100% speed	10 times with standard ball
100% speed	36 times with heavy ball	100% speed	36 times with heavy ball	100% speed	40 times with heavy ball	100% speed	40 times with heavy ball
100% speed	9 times with standard ball	100% speed	9 times with standard ball	100% speed	10 times with standard ball	100% speed	10 times with standard ball
Date: Day 1___ Day 2___ Day 3___		Date: Day 1___ Day 2___ Day 3___		Date: Day 1___ Day 2___ Day 3___		Date: Day 1___ Day 2___ Day 3___	

Week 5		Week 6		Week 7		Week 8	
75%-80% speed	Warm up 50 times with standard ball	75%-80% speed	Warm up 50 times with standard ball	75%-80% speed	Warm up 50 times with standard ball	75%-80% speed	Warm up 50 times with standard ball
100% speed	11 times with standard ball	100% speed	11 times with standard ball	100% speed	12 times with standard ball	100% speed	12 times with standard ball
100% speed	44 times with light ball	100% speed	46 times with light ball	100% speed	48 times with light ball	100% speed	48 times with light ball
100% speed	11 times with standard ball	100% speed	11 times with standard ball	100% speed	12 times with standard ball	100% speed	12 times with standard ball
Date: Day 1___ Day 2___ Day 3___		Date: Day 1___ Day 2___ Day 3___		Date: Day 1___ Day 2___ Day 3___		Date: Day 1___ Day 2___ Day 3___	

All throws are as hard as you can excluding warm up!

Figure 5.14 The weighted-ball workout program developed by Club K.

or partner takes a position in front of the pitcher, again permitting no slack in the tubing. As the pitcher strides forward, the coach or partner will have to draw his or her hand backward to keep the slack out of the tubing (see figure 15.15b). Again, the coach or partner can adjust the pressure he or she imparts to assist the leg drive forward but still must permit the pitcher to drive toe to heel and maintain mechanics. The pitcher should shadow pitch this drill, that is, not use a ball.

a

b

Figure 5.15 Using an ankle harness for *(a)* a resisted leg drive and *(b)* an assisted leg drive.

Full-body harness training should be done only with pitchers who have the physical integrity to withstand the forces imparted on the body. I do not recommend harnesses for young or inexperienced pitchers. The harness fits around the waist or midsection of the pitcher. The holder should stand in front of the pitcher and slightly off to the glove side, as shown in figure 5.16. (Note: the holder should try to stay close to the middle without getting into the path

Figure 5.16 Using a full-body harness. A fence or net can be substituted for a catcher.

of the ball, and the pitcher should use a flexible practice ball rather than a regulation hard softball, in case the holder gets hit). The purpose of the harness is to create momentum and eventually create muscle memory of that momentum. Essentially, the harness makes the stride more aggressive, in turn making the arm more aggressive and quicker. The full harness can also be used from behind to strengthen the body overall within the pitching motion itself.

THE FINAL PITCH

Pitchers fail to reach speed potentials for two main reasons: lack of effort and fear of losing control. These problems can usually be avoided early by not overemphasizing results and by encouraging younger pitchers to pitch aggressively with all their effort. Parents and coaches should be careful to not become obsessed with speed. Use drills to teach and help with effort and aggression, and be realistic about an athlete's potential.

Pitchers lack accuracy for two main reasons. One is simply a lack of consistency within the mechanics. As mentioned previously, when body parts are everywhere, you can expect the same result to occur with the location of the ball.

Mechanical problems such as restricted follow-throughs, posture compromises, and changing speeds can affect height consistency, whereas balance, power lines, and trunk or shoulder rotations can affect side-to-side consistency.

The other reason for lack of control is the absence of a focus point. Without a focus point, making adjustments is impossible. In addition, many pitchers are reluctant to adjust their focus point away from the target even when that focus point is failing to work.

Every hitter has at least one weakness. For some hitters, any pitch except one down the middle (red zone) is hard to handle. As the pitcher becomes proficient with her targets, her success rate will begin to climb. For beginners, simply moving the ball inside and outside, up and down will increase the number of strikeouts and decrease the number of hard hits.

Pitchers should strive to have a high percentage of accuracy on their targets and then use those location calls in a game. Pitchers and catchers should learn the colors of the zones and why and when they throw to a certain color. The coach should not always have to tell the pitcher and catcher what color to throw. For instance, if the pitch called is a fastball knee high and inside, the pitcher should know according to the count whether this pitch is yellow or green.

The pitcher should realize that if she falls behind in the count, she must throw more red pitches to avoid walking hitters. The more often pitchers are in the red, the more often and harder they will be hit. Pitchers who get ahead and stay ahead can throw more yellow and green pitches, increasing their strikeout frequency and overall success. One of the most valuable lessons a pitcher can learn is the importance of staying ahead in the count.

To conclude, remember that location will always be the pitcher's greatest asset. Without accuracy, the effectiveness of speed and movement is greatly reduced. Pinpoint accuracy at full speed is not luck and does not just happen. Consistency and correct fundamentals are the keys to high accuracy percentages.

Look at the following numbers: 374; 1,784; 15. Imagine trying to quickly arrive at a total for those three numbers if you did not understand the method of addition. You would probably guess incorrectly many times until finally, maybe, luckily, you happen to get it right. Using the method of addition, you simply stack up the three numbers, draw your line across the bottom, add the far right column, carry your one, and so on. The answer seems to come simply. You eliminate the incorrect guesses because you take the correct approach to the result.

Pitching is the same way. Without a method, achieving location and accuracy is nothing more than a guess, like trying to find a needle in a haystack. If the pitcher employs consistent mechanics and a plan (focus points and power lines), the correct results will follow.

PART II

EFFECTIVE MOVEMENT PITCH TECHNIQUE

For a beginner or an inexperienced pitcher, the goal of pitching is to get the ball into the strike zone. As a pitcher advances to higher levels, the goal is to keep the ball out of the strike zone. Simply missing the strike zone with every pitch, of course, would be easy, but to make it work and be a successful pitcher is anything but easy.

In progressing through the movement pitches, the pitcher goes through several different levels of learning. First, she must learn and understand the fundamentals involved in throwing the pitch. Second, with full motion and full speed she must be able to set body positions, find release points, and impart spin. After she accomplishes this, she can begin to experiment with the pitch during competition. Third, the pitcher will learn when to throw the pitches and to whom to throw them, and increase percentages of execution. Finally, to maximize effectiveness, the pitcher will learn to throw the pitch to different areas, or colors, of the strike zone, usually yellow and green.

PITCH LEARNING PROGRESSION

Naturally, everyone is eager to learn the movement pitches. Without good control over the fastball and solid fundamentals, however, the foundation will not support the structure. Moving on to movement pitches too soon can be frustrating and useless. If the pitcher cannot consistently release a pitch knee high, for example, learning a drop ball would be pointless because the release point is crucial to that pitch.

Most male pitchers will swear that fastpitch softball has only three pitches—up, down, and change. College coaches of the women's game will tell you that they have seen many pitchers be successful with the curve and screwball. Because of the nature of the underhand pitch and the fact that it is released level with the hip, the ball that changes planes aggressively, like the drop or the rise, has obvious advantages.

The curve and screw, however, often manage to fool hitters and have proved to be effective strikeout pitches. Furthermore, a good change-up can be the most lethal weapon in a pitcher's repertoire.

Assuming the foundation is set with a good base of fundamentals, the natural progression would be to either a drop ball or a change-up. If the pitcher has average or above-average speed, she should definitely go on to the change-up. The change-up will be the most effective complement to the fastball.

If the pitcher's speed is below average but she is ready to learn something new, she should go on to the peel drop ball. A change-up would not offer sufficient contrast to her normal-speed pitch, and the pitcher may not be strong enough to throw a change-up anyway. The peel drop will give her some downward movement and help prevent hitters from making frequent solid contact.

After having learned either the drop or the change-up, the one she passed over would be next. So if a pitcher has a fastball and learns a change-up, the drop ball would be a good choice for the next pitch. If the pitcher learned the drop first, she would go to the change-up next.

Following the drop and change-up, the rise ball would be the next pitch in line if the pitcher has the potential to be powerful. Steady average or above-average speed would indicate a powerful tendency. The rise ball, the most physically demanding pitch, requires a minimum speed of about 53 miles per hour to work. For that reason, along with the fact that the rise also presents a mental challenge, the pitcher should have some body awareness and a good work ethic. The rise ball requires a lot of patience and hard work.

The curveball and screwball usually serve as enhancement pitches, so pitchers often learn them last. It would be foolish, however, to underestimate the effectiveness of these pitches, which have been the dominant pitches for some extremely successful college, professional, and Olympic pitchers.

Some pitchers who struggle with the rise will adapt more easily to the curveball and use it as their dominant pitch. Obviously, curves and screws are good choices for jamming into or running away from hitters. Because the curve and screw do not make sudden plane changes, they are often most effective when moving out of the zone.

Although all pitches are more effective when moving out of the zone, the rise and drop typically yield a higher proportion of strikes when it is necessary to move the ball *through* the zone rather than *out of* the zone. When it is necessary for the pitcher to move the ball *through* the zone, the hitter can more easily read and anticipate curves and screws and will have greater success.

Let us look a little more closely at pitching *within* or *out of* the zone. Beginning pitchers use movement pitches only when they are ahead in the count. As soon as they get behind, they pump in the old fastball. Advanced pitchers, however, learn to use movement pitches no matter what the count. The difference is location. If the pitcher is behind in the count, the movement must stay *within* the zone, ending with a probable called strike if the hitter takes. If the pitcher is ahead in the count, the movement can travel *out of* the zone because the hitter must protect the plate and will be more likely to fish for a borderline pitch.

THE CPRS OF MOVEMENT

To attain *true movement* with any movement pitch, the pitcher must satisfy four requirements, known as the CPRS of movement:

Correct spin

Posture and weight shift

Release point

Speed of spin

Correct spin—With every pitch except the screwball, the ball should rotate toward the direction of the desired movement.

Posture and weight shift—Posture and weight shift, the most overlooked aspects of movement, are subtle but necessary and different for each pitch.

Release point—The pitcher must give the ball a chance to work. The release point will determine that opportunity. A ball cannot be thrown against the direction of desired movement. For example, the pitcher cannot release a drop ball on an upward trajectory and expect it to break back down in a distance of 35 to 38 feet.

Speed of spin—The speed at which the ball spins will dictate the severity of movement. Many pitchers believe that the speed of the pitch creates most of the movement when in fact it is the speed of the spin that causes the ball to move.

WHAT IT TAKES TO FOOL GOOD HITTERS

Nearly everywhere I go, parents come up to me and tell me the same story. Their daughter has lost her drop, or rise, or curve. "It was awesome last year and now it's just gone!" More than likely, the pitch is not gone. It's still there, and it's the same pitch it was last year. Something *is* different though—the hitters! The problem is that the hitters are not the same hitters they were last year.

The hitters are better, and that "curve" (really a fading outside fastball), or that "drop" (really a low fastball), or the "rise" (you guessed it—the high fastball) is not cutting it anymore. The hitters are either taking those pitches for balls or lighting them up for extra bases. The pitcher looks different because she is now throwing under more pressure with less ammunition.

For that reason, pitchers must get it right from the beginning, taking the time to learn pitches correctly from the start. They must understand that it takes time and hard work to master the precision required to produce *true* movement.

True movement is a cutting downward or across for the drop or curve, or the jump upward for the rise. True movement occurs suddenly as the ball approaches the hitter, not gradually throughout the pitch. The figure illustrates the difference between true movement and gradual movement.

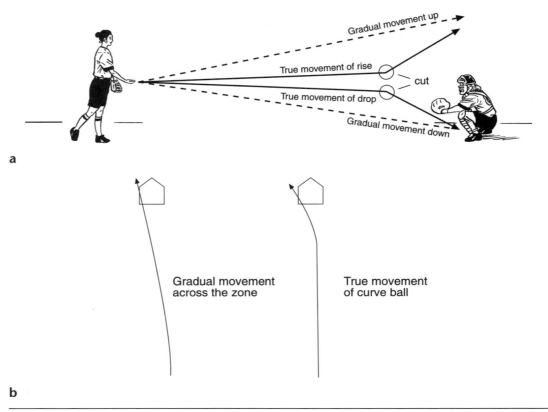

Compare *(a)* gradual movement and the true movement of the rise and drop, and *(b)* gradual movement and true movement of the curveball.

Throwing the change-up also requires more technique than the old trick of just slowing down the arm before release. The slow-down-the-arm method may work against poor or weak hitters, but good hitters will see the break in arm speed and read the pitch. To succeed at higher levels against good hitters, the pitcher will have to *sell* the change-up. If learned correctly, this sell should be a built-in part of the pitch.

Unlike the movement pitches, the change-up relies on deception of speed, not location. For that reason, the hitter must be fooled into believing the pitch is of normal velocity. Selling the change-up involves the appearance of both the pitch and the pitcher.

MAKING HONEST ASSESSMENTS

In talking with a pitcher and her parent or coach, I am often surprised at which pitches they believe the pitcher is throwing well. What I find more surprising and disappointing is to see that every pitch of the repertoire has the same spin and absolutely no sniff of proper technique.

The sad part about this scenario is that the pitcher will eventually hit a devastating wall. That wall will be the point when the parent says, "Well, she had it last year," or, "She threw great in league, but she just gets nervous in these tournaments."

Many parents want to give confidence to the pitcher by seeing movement that just isn't there. And, unfortunately, some pitching coaches want to give confidence to the check writer by teaching, or pretending to teach, three or four pitches in a couple of lessons. Or they teach the whole list of pitches when the pitcher does not yet have a single aspect of the first pitch correct. In the end the person who pays the price for all this deception is the athlete herself.

If you are a parent concerned with the best interest of your daughter or a coach who wants the best for your student, work with the pitcher for perfection and getting the pitches correct in the beginning.

If you talk to my students they will tell you that I am extremely particular, a nut for the details. I think the art of pitching and its demand for precision require the details to be tight and right. The pitcher should observe these guidelines to get the details right.

- She must insist on correct movements.
- She should use drills to reinforce the proper mechanics.
- She must not let pushy or overzealous parents rush the learning of pitches that she is not yet ready for.
- She must try to help herself. A time will come when she must be able to analyze and adjust on her own.

In the long run, the parent or coach who insists that the pitcher get the little things right will be serving the pitcher's best interest. Not much is worse than the plight of a 17-year-old who has the mental attitude and physical potential to be a college pitcher but not enough time to go back and learn the techniques she needs to compete at that level—not enough time to learn what she should have been mastering all along.

DROP BALL

6

The drop ball, pitched correctly, will give a pitcher many offensively uneventful innings throughout her career. Because of the location it is pitched to (the lower half of the legs), the drop is known for frustrating hitters by allowing them to contact only a fraction of the ball (usually the top half). This often prevents hitters from making the solid contact they desire.

The drop ball, when contacted, usually stays inside the park. The drop starts in the lower part of the zone and moves down from there. Contacting the top half of the ball rather than the middle or lower half is the recipe for hitting balls on the ground.

Contact on the middle or lower half will produce an upward or outward trajectory that allows the ball to carry. With lively bats and balls, along with 200-foot fences, it is precisely this upward and outward trajectory that college coaches are hoping to prevent. A good drop-ball pitcher is thus an attractive recruiting prospect.

CHARACTERISTICS AND EXPECTATIONS

The pitcher has two primary objectives for every hitter.

1. Get the strikeout. And if she doesn't get the strikeout, then
2. control the hitter

The drop ball lends itself handily to both the objectives. As previously mentioned, because the location of the drop is in the lower part of the zone and the movement is downward, the bat, when it makes contact, tends to hit the top side of the ball—yielding a ground ball. Solid hits off the drop tend to be line drives.

The drop knows no prejudice when it comes to speed. A slower pitcher can be extremely effective with the drop ball. This rule will not hold true with most other movement pitches, including the change-up.

PEEL DROP

Two methods can be used to impart the downward spin needed for the ball to cut or break sharply. These are known as the peel, or pull-up, drop and the turnover drop. The two pitches involve distinctly different techniques.

In teaching the drop ball to a pitcher who has never thrown one, I almost always teach the peel drop first. Because the peel drop is faster and does not typically risk injury even with a mistake, the peel is always the first drop pitch that a younger pitcher (under 14 years old) should learn. After some experience, they may choose to switch spin methods.

In throwing the peel drop, the pitcher imparts spin by simply snapping the ball or peeling the ball off the end of the fingertips, as shown in figure 6.1. If the pitcher's fastball mechanics are correct, the peel-drop spin is already there. The

Figure 6.1 With the peel drop, the ball peels off the end of the fingertips.

only addition may be a little more emphasis on the snap at release to maximize the speed of spin. Some pitchers choose to finish the follow-through upward on the drop instead of outward like the fastball (see figure 6.2). Either follow-through will work well.

The four-seam grip (C grip) is usually recommended, but the two-seam grip (horseshoe) can also be used. As with the fastball, the C grip will go straight downward, and the horseshoe may tend to tail slightly while going downward. As long as she can control the pitch, the pitcher should use the grip that is more comfortable and yields the best result.

TURNOVER DROP

The second type of drop, the turnover, is more difficult to learn for three reasons:

- More body awareness is required to master the movements.
- The turnover drop works better with faster speeds. The turnover will help a faster pitcher maintain good cuts. For slower pitchers, however, the decrease in speed off the fastball (which is inevitable) often has a negative effect on a pitcher already at a speed disadvantage.
- Making mistakes with the turnover drop can cause injury to the pitcher.

A coach should carefully consider these issues before first teaching the turnover to an inexperienced drop-ball pitcher.

a   b

Figure 6.2   Some pitchers finish the follow-through (*a*) upward instead of (*b*) outward as with the fastball.

To gain downward spin on the turnover drop, the pitcher does exactly what the name implies. Rather than let the ball roll off the fingertips, she turns the ball downward by turning her hand over the top of the ball. This detour from letting the ball roll off the fingertips costs the pitcher some speed on the drop ball. This loss of speed can be as slight as 2 or 3 miles per hour or as much as 8 or 10 miles per hour, depending on the pitcher's experience and comfort in throwing the pitch.

Whatever the exact amount, the pitcher should expect some decrease as she veers from the biomechanics of speed. Usually, but not always, the decrease in speed is noticeable only by the radar gun. In other words, the pitch does not appear to be, or is not intended to be, an off-speed pitch.

To technically break down the spin of the turnover drop a bit more: the pitcher has her hand underneath the ball with the fingers pointing away from the body as she nears her hip with the arm circle (see figure 6.3a). At the release point, the hand comes from underneath the ball and rolls over the top, thus imparting a downward spin (see figure 6.3b). The follow-through of the hand is downward and loose.

With the turnover drop the pitcher may make the mistake of believing that she is underneath the ball when (because of muscle memory) she is really behind or slightly on top of the ball, as with the fastball, rise, curve, screw,

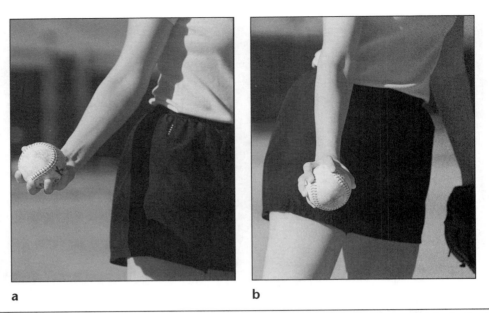

a   b

Figure 6.3 For the turnover drop spin, *(a)* the pitcher's hand is underneath the ball with the fingers pointing away from the body as the arm circle nears the hip, and then *(b)* the hand moves over the ball at release.

and some change-ups (see figure 6.4a). When the time comes to turn the ball over at the release point, the pitcher feels as if she is turning it over but instead is really going *around* the ball (see figure 6.4b). This action throws the elbow outward and places the arm in an awkward and dangerous position for the back side of the shoulder, specifically the group of muscles that make up the rotator cuff. The resulting injury can be serious.

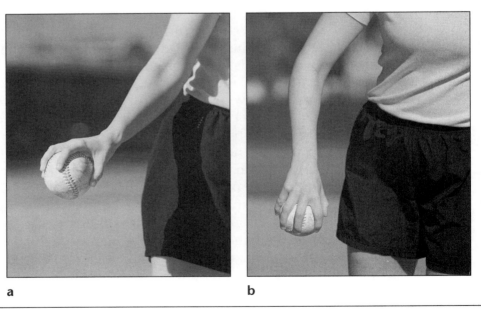

a   b

Figure 6.4 A common mistake happens when *(a)* the pitcher's hand is behind or slightly on top of the ball, and *(b)* at release the hand goes around the ball, instead of turning it over.

Another injury can occur simply by learning the pitch incorrectly. Some coaches encourage pitchers to raise their shoulders or "pop the shoulder upward" to get the hand over the ball (see figure 6.5). This unnecessary, dangerous move places stress on the shoulder joint itself. *Placing spin on the ball is always performed by snapping the wrist.* The upper arm has nothing to do with imparting spin on the ball. Coaches and pitchers should focus largely on what happens from the elbow down in working on correct spins.

When learning the movements required of the turnover and committing those movements to muscle memory, the pitcher should use a Spinner to see the results clearly. It is often difficult to see the spin when using a ball. The pitcher should start out close (5 feet away) on one knee

Figure 6.5 Popping the shoulder upward places stress on the shoulder joint.

and gradually back up, as shown in figure 6.6. After she masters the spin from one knee at 20 feet, she should come back up close and stand up. She may want to leave out the full circle to begin and use just the rock-back approach.

Figure 6.6 Using the Spinner from a one-knee position.

Remember that the elbow stays close to the body when the pitch is thrown correctly. If the pitcher makes the mistake of spinning around the ball, the elbow will fly outward, as in figure 6.7.

The turnover drop is a safe pitch if executed correctly. Injuries occur during the learning process through ignorance or by not paying enough attention to details. This pitch sometimes gets a bad rap because coaches and pitchers do not understand its fundamentals. When performed correctly, the turnover drop does not present an injury risk.

POSTURE AND WEIGHT SHIFT

As I mentioned at the outset of this section, posture and weight shift are the most overlooked aspects of the movement pitches. Most pitchers work on getting a specific grip, then maybe a spin, and after that believe they have all it takes to make the ball move.

Figure 6.7 The elbow flying outward.

According to the laws of physics, what goes up must come down. With that in mind, realize that all pitches will eventually drop regardless of the release point, or anything else for that matter. But in fastpitch softball, we want the ball to drop *before* it reaches the hitter. Hence, we need to consider posture and weight shift. These two factors determine not only when the ball will drop but also how high the pitcher can release the ball and still get the pitch to work.

We discussed earlier, in the examination of the fastball, the need for the posture to be straight and tall. To get the intended result from the drop ball, the pitcher must shift all her weight to her stride (or front) leg before the release point, as shown in figure 6.8. Also, in shifting her weight, the pitcher should position her body with a slight lean forward. The key word here is *lean*. The head should be positioned over the top of the stride foot. The pitcher should not bend at the waist because doing so would cause some of her weight to stay back and not commit completely to the stride leg.

To gain downward trajectory, the pitcher should release the ball at an angle. If the angle is set without the weight shift, and at regular stride position, the pitching arm will be lower to the ground at release and the starting point of the ball will then be considerably lower at the outset.

Figure 6.8 The ideal drop-ball posture.

If the downward trajectory is imparted by the angle of the body, accomplished by a posture lean and weight shift forward, the height of the pitch is at its maximum. This positioning allows the pitcher to release the ball higher into the legs of the hitter if necessary.

To shift the weight to the front foot, it is extremely helpful for the pitcher to shorten the length of the stride. When initially learning the drop, she should shorten the stride considerably just to see the correct results of the pitch. After experiencing some success, she can begin to polish the pitch by gradually lengthening the stride.

The stride for the drop ball, however, usually will not equal the stride for the other pitches. The restriction in the length of the stride can help increase the effectiveness of the pitch. But the important points are that the weight shifts to the front foot before release and the head is located over the front foot.

A common mistake occurs when the pitcher is late in shifting the weight and setting the posture position. Even top pitchers fall victim to this error. The mistake occurs when the pitcher lands on the stride foot and does not land in the correct position (see figure 6.9). She then tries to get to the correct position before release. This will never work. *The pitcher must be positioned correctly when the stride foot lands.* Otherwise, the body will be behind the ball at release, causing the pitch to hang in the strike zone.

Because of the posture and weight shift, the pitcher will most likely fall forward after release. She can allow this to happen but then must regain balance and defensive position quickly.

Figure 6.9 Incorrect drop-ball position at the stride-foot land.

Corrections to Drop Posture

In short, the posture position of the drop will be the most difficult mechanical aspect to learn. Remember that the stride leg stays underneath the torso of the pitcher on the drop, rather than in front of the body as with the fastball. Also, if the pitcher can think of the fastball as moving the body *to* the front leg at completion of the pitch, she should imagine the drop ball as moving the body *through* the front leg.

The batter can take three positions within the batter's box—up, middle, or back. The pitcher should adjust the severity of her weight shift and posture according to where the hitter locates herself. If the hitter is in front of the box, the pitcher will have to get to the front foot more quickly and slightly exaggerate the posture forward. To do this, she may have to use a stride shorter than her normal drop stride. If the hitter is in the back of the box, the weight shift and lean can be subtler. At any rate, a hitter should not be able to eliminate the effectiveness of the pitch simply by changing her location in the batter's box.

Many pitchers learn a generic drop ball. By generic, I mean a ball that drops at the same place and is released at the same point every time. These pitchers throw the same pitch no matter where the hitter moves in the box and no matter what the count is. They will have limited effectiveness when facing smart hitters or coaches. If a pitcher is unable to change the variables when necessary, hitters can render the pitch ineffective.

When the pitch does not work, pitchers must learn to analyze and adjust. Two things can go wrong with the drop.

- The pitch can be released at the correct height and not move.
- The pitch can be released too high or too low.

If the pitcher releases the ball at the correct height but the ball does not move, she either shifted her weight incorrectly or did not set her posture correctly or in time. The pitcher must find a way to shift her weight sooner. Shortening the step can be a quick fix to this problem, but the pitcher must be aware of where the head is landing.

If the pitcher releases the ball too high or too low, she should refocus to adjust the height of the pitch. After fixing the height, she can assess posture and weight shift.

A problem that occurs almost exclusively with the turnover drop causes the pitch to move outside and not drop. At the point when the pitcher should be turning the ball over, she initiates the move with the shoulder rather than the wrist (see figure 6.10). This causes the shoulders to spin (somewhat like a helicopter blade) and straightens the pitcher's posture. The ball then moves across the zone, not downward. The glove-side shoulder should remain toward the catcher until the follow-through, at which point the shoulders will square. The throwing-arm shoulder should never lead the body.

a   b   c

Figure 6.10 In this sequence, the pitcher initiates the move with the shoulder instead of the wrist.

Posture Drills

Here are a few of my favorite drills for the drop ball.

One-Leg Drill

This drill places the pitcher in exactly the position she will land when she sets the stride foot. The pitcher places the stride foot under herself with all her weight over the leg. She bends the knee slightly so that the stride leg accepts the weight and is flexible. Her head should be slightly over the front foot. She can allow the back toe to touch the ground lightly for balance (see figure 6.11).

The pitcher can bounce and move around some at first to become comfortable with the position. From this position, she makes the full circle, maintaining the position and releasing the ball at knee height. After release, the body will follow through forward in the direction of the ball. She should not try to balance.

Figure 6.11 Correct position for the one-leg drill.

If the pitcher correctly sets the position and holds it throughout the pitch, she will see instant results when she releases the ball at the correct point. She should perform the drill at half speed, focusing only on body awareness.

As the pitcher begins to experience steady success with this drill, she can add the step. At stride, the pitcher should try to get back into the position of the one-leg drill as soon as possible. She stays at half speed at first but gradually adds speed as she has success. She must remember, however, to set the positions more quickly as she adds arm speed.

Mound Drill

Using a baseball pitcher's mound, the pitcher starts with the one-leg drill first, then gradually adds the step and arm speed (see figure 6.12). By throwing off the incline, the pitcher can more easily set and feel the angles of the body, thus developing correct muscle memory. She must remember to land with the stride leg *underneath* the body.

Rope Drill

Using a rope or string positioned about five feet in front of the plate, as shown in figure 6.13, the pitcher pitches drop balls over the top of the rope. If the

Figure 6.12 Using a baseball mound.

Figure 6.13 For the rope drill, the pitcher pitches drop balls over a rope positioned about five feet in front of the plate.

pitches are thrown correctly, the ball will go over the rope and drop below it by the time it reaches the catcher. This drill provides the pitcher an excellent gauge of cut location and severity.

Rope height can be changed with this drill for variations of count, either ahead or behind (yellow or green). If the pitcher is behind in the count (yellow), the rope should be held higher. If the pitcher is ahead in the count (green), the

Figure 6.14 Hitter's locations and consequent catcher's locations: *(a)* regular, *(b)* moved backward, and *(c)* moved forward.

rope can be held lower. The rope can also be moved forward or backward to represent a move by the hitter up or back in the box. The cut should take place immediately after the ball crosses over the rope. The pitcher can experiment with getting onto the leg quicker and notice the effect that has on the cut. *The catcher must move forward and backward when the hitter does* (see figure 6.14).

RELEASE POINT

The release point for the drop ball must be equal to or below the pitcher's hand at the time the ball is released. For instance, if the pitcher's hand at the release of the ball is thigh high, she can release the ball anywhere at or below that point.

The typical release point for the drop ball is knee high to the hitter. In getting more technical with location, there are really three possibilities: exactly knee high, slightly above the knee and breaking within the zone, or slightly below the knee and breaking completely out of the zone. The magic rule is that the pitch cannot be thrown against the direction it is intended to break. The pitcher must place the ball in the proper environment to allow it to make its move.

THE FINAL PITCH

The drop ball is sometimes difficult to practice. For one thing, no one likes to catch a ball in the dirt. The simple truth is that in learning the drop ball, many pitches will go into the dirt, and once the pitcher masters the drop, many strikeouts will be chalked up from balls in the dirt.

I have heard parents, when catching, tell the pitcher to "keep the ball up." This is exactly what we do not want them to do. I have seen games in which no drops are called "because the catcher doesn't like them." In other games no drops are called when a runner gets on base "because we don't want to risk a passed ball."

When pitchers learn to pitch, catchers must also learn to catch. A catcher's technique can make or break many pitches, and the drop ball is no exception. The catcher's method of framing the low ones and blocking the balls in the dirt will be crucial to the pitcher's success.

The coach must create a friendly environment in which the pitcher can make mistakes without severe consequences. Pitchers and catchers should practice with flexible or softer practice balls that possess the qualities of a real ball without causing bruises and bumps when the ball misses the glove.

CHANGE-UP

7

The change-up is arguably the most important weapon in a pitcher's arsenal. The deception of the change-up is in its alteration of speed, not its location or movement. This makes the change-up a unique pitch, since all other pitches rely primarily on the deception of location or movement.

The truth about the whole thing is this. If a hitter swings hard at the rise ball and misses for strike three, she may not be happy about it, but at least she can return to the dugout with a little bit of pride. After all, she swung right with the ball. It was just higher than her bat. But if a hitter swings hard at the change-up for strike three (or any other strike for that matter), the pride thing works against her. There is no pride in swinging a second or two before the pitch even arrives, or flailing helplessly at the ball as it passes, or worst of all, watching a pitch slow enough for Grandma to hit float right down Broadway for a called strike! Any of those results is simply embarrassing, and if it happens enough, extremely frustrating.

Hitting is eye-hand coordination and timing. Hitters work long hours to sharpen their timing. When they get to the park and prepare for the game, they study the pitcher's speed and begin the process of timing the swing. A pitcher with an effective change-up presents hitters with a difficult timing adjustment. Lump that together with the embarrassment factor, and the change-up becomes a pitch that many hitters dread.

CHARACTERISTICS AND EXPECTATIONS

The change-up is technically a pitch that is at least 15 miles per hour slower than the fastest pitch of the given pitcher. The change-up could be as slow as half the velocity of the pitcher's fastest pitch. The pitcher should avoid becoming hung up on an exact speed. She should instead focus on the effectiveness of the pitch itself and accomplishing its fundamental goals.

The three fundamental goals of the change-up are to

- maintain full arm speed,
- keep the path of the ball on a straight line, and
- locate the ball in the strike zone.

Many young pitchers learn a change-up by simply reducing their arm speed before releasing the ball. Against very young hitters or poor hitters, this technique will work fine. Against hitters of fair ability or those beginning to mature in the game, this technique will lead to extra-base hits.

Some pitchers who learn the slow-the-arm technique at a young age find it a difficult habit to break. Therefore, if a pitcher is pitching fast enough to learn a change-up, I encourage her to learn one that will continue to be effective, no matter what level of hitter she faces. When choosing a particular change-up, the pitcher should find one that at full distance and full speed will be comfortable without a decrease in arm speed.

Second, the change-up should follow a straight path toward the target. By straight, I mean flat—without an arch or hump in the middle. At the point where the hitter makes up her mind whether to swing or not (about halfway from the pitcher to the plate), the ball *must* be located in an area that the hitter recognizes as a future strike.

Look at figure 7.1. If the pitch has even a slight hump to it, the batter will read its location at the decision point as out of the strike zone, causing her initially to hold up on her swing. As the ball descends downward and into the zone, the hitter will realize that the pitch is a change-up and still have time to load and unload!

Coaches and parents often tell me that the change-up of a given pitcher is too slow when that is not the problem at all. The scenario of the hump is taking place, and because the hitter holds, then loads and swings, the coach or parent assumes that the hitter read the pitch out of the hand as a change-up. Many times that is not the case. The hitter simply read the pitch as out of the strike zone and held her swing. If the pitcher can flatten out the pitch, she will see different results. To go a step further, I would rather see a change-up that is flat and falls short of the plate than one that arches and gets to the catcher.

Finally, a good change-up should be thrown predominately as a strike. If all the hitter has to do is somehow hold up the swing and wait for the umpire to call the pitch a ball, the change-up will not be effective. Many younger pitchers put too much emphasis on hitting an exact location, such as knee

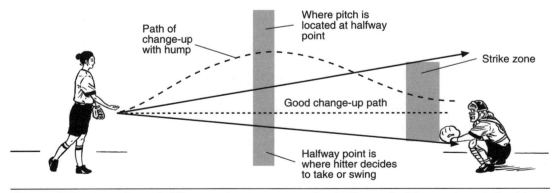

Figure 7.1 Location of different change-ups at the halfway decision point of the hitter. Straight lines indicate the complete area of a strike on its path to the catcher.

high on the outside corner. So you have a pitcher throw a beautiful change-up that freezes the hitter, but the umpire sees it as being just off the corner and calls it a ball. What a waste! The pitcher must put that pitch in the zone and work hard on selling it to the hitter as a full-speed pitch.

TYPES OF CHANGE-UPS

There are many ways to throw a change-up. The pitcher should experiment with a few and find one that best fits her particular style that she can sell to the hitter once she masters it. If the pitcher is to accomplish the goal of maintaining full arm speed while cutting significant speed from the pitch, she will have to hinder some other speed factors, primarily wrist snap or follow-through.

Most types of change-ups require some type of grip adjustment. The reason for adjusting grips is to attempt to limit wrist snap and whip, which will in turn limit speed. The pitcher must remember this as the goal of the grip and not be fooled into believing that the grip by itself will make the change-up work. Usually, she will adjust or limit the follow-through as well. By using these two factors, the pitcher can adjust the speed of the ball without decelerating the arm at release.

The following is a sample of three popular change-ups: the turnaround change, the shove change, and the knuckleball.

Turnaround Change

Grip. For the turnaround change-up, the pitcher should use a normal grip as far as tightness goes. An excessively tight grip will prohibit the wrist from spinning quickly. Some pitchers like to grip the horseshoe and get a little fade or wiggle at the end. The grip, as you will see, is not what limits the speed of this pitch.

Description.   The pitcher starts the circle normally and stays normal until the lower side of the back of the circle (approximately eight o'clock for a right-hander). At this point, the pitcher flips her wrist totally around, causing the back of the hand to lead toward the catcher (see figure 7.2a). The path of the hand should leave the circle out front and head directly for the catcher (see figure 7.2b). The palm should stay downward and not flip up at release. Although flipping is a natural tendency, this action should be avoided because it will tend to put the dreaded hump on the path of the pitch. The catcher should never see the pitcher's palm. At the release point, the pitcher should just open the hand and let the pitch pop out toward the catcher (see figure 7.2c).

This pitch will go slow because of the limitation put on the wrist snap (by turning the wrist backward) and follow-through (by not snapping the wrist through the ball at the end, but simply letting it pop out).

Drills.   The pitcher should practice the following drills for the turnaround change.

a

b

c

Figure 7.2 The turnaround change: *(a)* the back of the hand is toward the catcher at the lower side of the back of the circle; *(b)* the path of the hand extends forward at the release point; *(c)* the pitcher opens her hand and lets the pitch pop out toward the catcher.

The pitcher starts one stride away from a bucket. (The pitcher should match her arm speed to her distance but keep steady arm speed throughout the circle. For example, if she is pitching from half of full distance, her arm speed should be half of full effort and start and stay at that speed throughout the circle. The pitcher must not start fast and then slow down the arm.) At a slow but steady speed the pitcher goes around to eight o'clock and turns the wrist, continues past the hip, and reaches to the catcher, or in this case, over the bucket. As the pitcher extends her pitching hand and the ball over the bucket, she drops the ball into the bucket (see figure 7.3). At release, the

Figure 7.3 Extending the hand and dropping the ball into the bucket.

arm and hand should be no higher than the pitcher's waist, and the palm should always be facing downward.

The pitcher continues this turn, reach, and drop sequence until it starts to look natural. She can easily practice this alone. Gradually, as the pitcher starts to get things consistently right, she can back up one step at a time. As she backs up, she can add a bit of speed each step. At about halfway, the catcher becomes part of the drill, catching the balls, throwing them back, and reminding the pitcher to visualize dropping the pitch into the bucket. *The only difference in pitching from 5 feet away and 40 feet away is arm speed.*

Shove Change

Grips. The shove change can be gripped in several different ways. Some pitchers simply draw the ball into the pad of the hand and squeeze tight. Some pitchers use a circle grip by curling the index finger around the side of the ball (see figure 7.4a). Still others tuck a single knuckle to imitate another grip, such as the rise or curve. The goal of the grip is to stabilize the wrist and prevent a loose wrist snap at release. Some pitchers can do this on their own, allowing them to use any grip. Other pitchers need some help in tightening the wrist, making it necessary for them to tighten the grip, tuck a knuckle or two, or grip the ball deeper in the hand (see figure 7.4b).

Figure 7.4 Two common ways to grip the ball for the shove change: *(a)* a circle grip with the index finger curled around the side of the ball, and *(b)* gripping the ball deeper in the hand.

Description. Again, the pitcher starts the circle normally. At approximately eight o'clock (for a right-hander), the pitcher allows the ball to come first in a shoving manner. We learned earlier that the whip occurs at the bottom of the circle with the elbow leading the whipping action. This huge speed factor is what the pitcher is attempting to eliminate by putting the ball first. Compare the two methods in figure 7.5. Essentially, instead of whipping the ball through the bottom of the circle, the pitcher pushes it through to the catcher. The follow-through again goes directly toward the catcher, and the hand simply opens up to let the ball pop out. The pitcher should try not to let the ball roll off the fingers, but instead allow it to pop off the hand at release. The fingers should open up and stay out of the way. The hand and arm should be about waist high at release.

Drills. The pitcher should use the following strategies to practice the shove change.

PRACTICE IT Again, she starts close and very slowly with steady arm speed (see figure 7.6a). Instead of using a full circle, she draws the elbow back and pushes the ball outward. This is not exactly a rock back because the ball is in front of the elbow, being pushed instead of extended in a rocking manner. (The pitcher can imagine drawing back an arrow underhand or punching someone in the stomach.) At close distances (until about halfway back) if the draw back and pop-out release are done correctly, the ball will have little or no spin. As the pitcher begins to back up, the ball will gain spin, but she should remember the goal of shoving the ball throughout. The pitcher should continue to back up with no circle until just past halfway. At this point, if her technique is correct and the ball has little or no spin, she can return to short-distance pitching and

a   b

Figure 7.5   Compare these two methods: *(a)* the elbow first as in correct mechanics and *(b)* the ball first as in the shove change-up.

add the circle. She repeats the gradual backing-up process until reaching full distance and full speed (see figure 7.6b).

The pitcher may need weeks to master this drill, but she should not rush the advancement backward. If the pitcher rushes to throw the full distance before she is ready, the wrist snap will take over. This will be a difficult habit to break if she does not conquer it at the beginning.

Knuckleball

Grips.   Unlike its baseball counterpart, the grip of the softball is usually with the fingertips digging into the ball rather than with the knuckles themselves. The pitcher may choose to dig in all the fingers or any variation of fingers (see examples in figure 7.7), but the key is to keep the *fingerprint* of any finger off the ball. The fingerprints themselves tend to impart spin, making the pitch difficult to master. For this reason, if a finger is not digging, it is better to roll it into the palm and keep it totally off the surface of the ball. Due to size of the ball and the pitcher's hand, loose fingers will sometimes rest on the ball. Be sure they are resting and not gripping.

a   b

Figure 7.6   *(a)* First, start slowly and close to home, then *(b)* gradually back up to full distance and full speed.

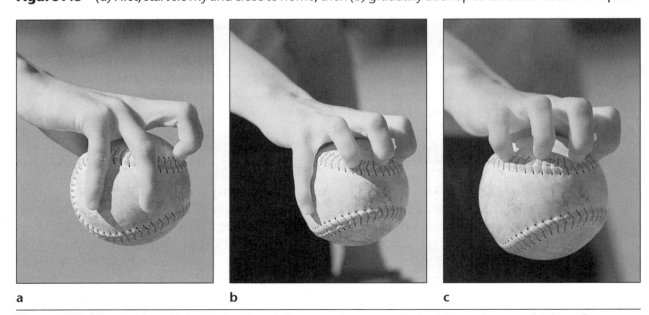

a   b   c

Figure 7.7   For the knuckleball grip, the pitcher can choose to dig in *(a)* two fingers, *(b)* three fingers, or *(c)* four fingers.

Description.   The limited grip of the knuckleball will in turn limit the wrist snap. As with the shove change, the ball leads the elbow through the bottom of the circle instead of vice versa. At release, the pitcher either opens the fingers and pushes the ball off the fingertips or simply allows the ball to leave on its own by lifting the thumb. The follow-through goes directly toward the release point. The ball should have little or no spin and should dance on its pathway to the catcher, at the mercy of whatever air currents are present.

Drills.   The pitcher should practice the knuckleball with the following drills and routines.

PRACTICE IT   Because of the size of the female hand and the size of the ball, for most pitchers the grip will tend to be uncomfortable. For this reason, the pitcher should simply begin to sit around with a ball in her hand and become accustomed to the tightness and discomfort that she will initially experience.

From here, the pitcher can take the ball without a circle and toss it upward to herself (see figure 7.8). Doing this will allow her to feel the opening of the fingers and thumb and at a basic level start to master throwing the ball without spin. After learning to self-toss the ball with no spin, the pitcher starts close to the catcher without using a circle. She moves back over time as she masters throwing from the current distance. At just past halfway (see figure 7.9), she returns to close distance and adds the circle. The pitcher may want to add the circle with a self-toss first before tossing to the catcher.

Figure 7.8   The pitcher practices tossing the ball to herself to get used to the release of the knuckle ball.

Figure 7.9   After gradually backing up and throwing without the circle, start using the circle about halfway back.

DISTANCE AND SPEED

Once again, pitchers must be patient in the progression of distance and speed. They should stay close to the target and repeat correctly as much as possible. I have pitchers who learn the turnaround change-up into a bucket in one lesson. In a few days they are throwing it from 40 feet away. And do you know what those pitchers are doing from 40 feet away? They are snapping the heck out of their wrists, following through at the top of the circle, and putting humps and speed on the ball like crazy! In other words, their mechanics are completely wrong. By rushing to pitch the full distance they have made habits of their mistakes.

When learning or warming up the change-up, the pitcher should always start close. She should have goals at one-quarter distance, one-half distance, three-quarters distance, and the full distance. For instance, at one-quarter distance, the pitcher may omit the circle and just try to get a feel for the correct release. At half distance, she includes the circle and adds more speed, and her back side starts to imitate a faster pitch. (Often, the tendency is to lunge out on the stride foot on the change-up and forget the back-side mechanics. The pitcher must use the proper mechanics when adding distance to the pitch.) At three-quarters distance, the effort approaches her maximum. This is a good place to check balance. The head must be under control, not forward or off to the side, to maintain accuracy. Finally, at full distance, the correct mechanics must be in place. Effort on speed and the arm circle should be all out at this point.

PRACTICE IT

One-Knee Drill

A great drill for practicing alone is to kneel down on one knee about five feet away from the target (see figure 7.10). The target could be a box, a stool tipped over, or just some tape on the wall or in the net. From one knee in a stabilized position, the pitcher performs the correct mechanics with the pitching arm. The drill allows the pitcher to think her way through the correct movements and create muscle memory with those movements.

When the correct mechanics start to become more of a habit, the pitcher can challenge herself by reducing the target in width (8 to 12 inches) and height (waist high and lower). She can also begin to back up and add arm speed. But she should not go past three-quarters distance without adding the help of the lower body. The player can continue the drill from a standing position, again starting close and working all the way back.

Figure 7.10 For the one-knee drill, start from about five feet from the target and gradually back up. Be sure to line up the knee and stride foot to the target.

Rope Drill

In this drill the pitcher starts at half distance with a rope about 5 feet in front of the catcher. The rope should be $3\frac{1}{2}$ to 4 feet high (see figure 7.11). The goal of the pitcher is to keep the ball *under* the rope. With the rope at the halfway point, any humps will cause the ball to be above the rope. As the pitcher adds speed and backs up, the rope should always stay at the halfway point between the pitcher and the catcher. The rope will be a good visual reminder to the pitcher, even during a game. She must put the ball under the rope.

Figure 7.11 The pitcher tries to keep the ball under a rope positioned halfway between the pitcher and catcher.

CHANGE-UP CHECKPOINTS

Remember that the key to a good change-up is the appearance of normalcy; the pitch must look like any other regular-speed pitch. To accomplish this, the pitcher, catcher, and coach must have a sharp eye and keen awareness of the look of the pitch. A useful practice is to break down the pitch into three categories and check them one at a time.

First, the pitcher warms up the change-up. She then chooses a regular-speed pitch to mix with it. Most pitchers choose their fastball because it usually calls for the most effort speedwise, but the mix pitch can be any pitch with velocity. The pitcher alternately throws fastballs and change-ups, *focusing only on the front side* of the arm circle. She and the catcher and coach watch the grip, wind-up, and circle up to the top on the fastball first, and then watch the same aspects of the change-up. Is the windup just as aggressive? Does the grip appear to be tighter on the change-up? Is the break from the glove and up the circle the same? She should repeat this sequence for 10 to 12 pitches.

Next, the pitcher, catcher, and coach *check the back side of the circle* and past the hip to release. Again, the pitcher throws the fastball and change-up on alternate pitches. Is the speed of the arm slowing near the hip on the change-up? Does the pitcher attempt to stop at the end, or does she continue smoothly through the release? Is the shove or turnaround smooth? Is an adjusted grip visible at any time throughout the pitch?

Finally, they *check the back-leg drive* in the alternating of the fastball and change-up. Does the leg come through aggressively? Does a lagging leg drive compromise posture? Is the finish balanced and in control?

After checking each of the three areas individually, they put it all together at the end. Bystanders can be asked to identify any obvious differences. The pitcher should try to feel the total pitch effort with both the change-up and the fastball.

DETECTING THE CHANGE-UP IN A RANDOM MIX

Videotape offers another way to check the match of a velocity pitch and the change-up. The pitcher warms up both pitches completely and begins mixing. The coach or a helper sets up a video camera in one of the batter's boxes to capture the view of the hitter. I prefer to place the camera on the throwing-arm side of the pitcher to obtain a full view of the hand and arm. Instead of a set pattern, such as every other pitch being a change-up, the pitcher randomly mixes the fastball and change-up. For instance, she may throw two fastballs and a change-up, then one fastball and three change-ups, then one fastball and one change-up, and so on.

The pitcher should put away the tape for a few days (long enough to forget any of the sequence) and then take a look at it to see if she can detect when she will throw the change-up by a difference in arm speed, grip, effort, form, and so on. Catchers and coaches can also join this session, looking for signs as if they were opposing players or coaches.

THE FINAL PITCH

The pitcher should choose the change-up that works best with her particular delivery. What works for one pitcher may not work at all for another pitcher. Experimenting with the various kinds of change-ups is fine, but the goal should be to find one that works and then to stick with it.

Control should not be the initial priority. The pitcher may need a couple of years to develop a change-up that she can blend naturally into her pitching sequence and throw with accuracy. From the beginning, however, fundamentals must be a priority. The pitcher must not allow mistakes such as wrist snapping and follow-throughs to become habits just because she is not seeing the negative effects from 10 feet away.

The pitcher should seek perfection in mechanics and a natural, smooth appearance. As with the fundamentals of the fastball, after the pitcher has mastered the mechanics, she can move on to location. The number-one goal of the change-up is to sell the pitch to the hitter. I would much rather have a great sell on a pitch in the dirt than a lousy sell on a pitch down the middle. The first one is a ball; the second one is a double.

Throwing a good change-up requires full effort. For example, if the pitcher is throwing the shove change-up correctly, she will need to use every bit of her effort and strength to get the ball to the catcher. She has removed the speed factors of whipping the arm and following through the pitch, therefore requiring maximum effort to reach the distance. She should keep her level of effort in mind when progressing backward on a change-up. If it suddenly becomes easy to reach the target, she should check for wrist snaps and follow-throughs, and perhaps move a step or two closer for a while.

I often hear pitchers say that they were doing a light workout so they "just threw some change-ups." I do not understand that statement. Change-ups, thrown correctly, are the most physically demanding pitches of all. The pitcher must maintain full arm speed and physical effort while using techniques that prevent the body from throwing the ball fast.

RISE BALL

The rise ball is undoubtedly a dominant pitch in fastpitch softball. Because the pitch climbs upward, it is difficult to track and anticipate. Known as a power pitch, its trademark is the letter *K*. An effective rise ball can establish a pitcher's reputation and put her on the road to success.

The rise ball, however, has a down side: it usually passes through the power zone of the hitter. Although the pitch often results in strikes, this is usually the pitch that will travel farthest when the hitter makes contact. So, ironically, the pitch that helps pitchers produce strikes is also the one that helps hitters produce home runs.

CHARACTERISTICS AND EXPECTATIONS

Many pitchers who claim to have the rise ball fail to accomplish even the first requirement—spinning the ball backward. The backward spin of the rise ball is usually the most difficult spin for females to master. The spin requires the hand to pass directly under the ball with precision and quickness.

Another prerequisite to mastering the spin of the rise ball is the sheer strength and quickness of the hand and forearm. The ball must move upward, resisting gravity, so it requires not only correct spin but very fast spin. For this reason, the pitcher must be physically mature to have even the potential to execute the rise ball. Because of the difficult movements required, body awareness and mental maturity will also be beneficial.

The pitch is released on a slightly upward angle, and the spin takes over from there. In relation to the speed of the spin, the ball will often appear to jump or hop to a higher level. This sudden change of level is what makes the anticipation and tracking of the pitch so difficult for the hitter.

GRIPS

As with every movement pitch, the major factor in accomplishing spin is the wrist snap. The grip is a way to help with the snap or speed up the spin, but the grip in and of itself will not cause the ball to spin backward. The correct movement of the forearm, wrist, and fingers will determine the angle of the spin.

To throw the rise, the hand must pass underneath the softball in a straight path toward the target, thus imparting a backward spin onto the ball (see figure 8.1). A common mistake occurs when the ball leaves the side of the index finger. Instead of a backward spin, a vertical right-to-left spin is imparted (see figure 8.2). This mistake can be caused either by the path of the arm or the angle of the wrist snap.

To help avoid this type of spin, pitchers should use one of two common grips. Both use the index finger to block the ball from leaving off the side of the hand and guide it instead to allow the hand to pass directly under. One grip tucks or digs the index finger into the cover of the ball (see figure 8.3a); the other rolls the index finger along the side (see figure 8.3b).

The tuck or dig places the middle finger along a seam of the ball. The index finger digs into the cover with the pressure on the inside tip of the index finger. At release, the index finger should push out and upward on the ball, causing the ball to be forced off the back of the hand. The follow-through can finish as low as the waist

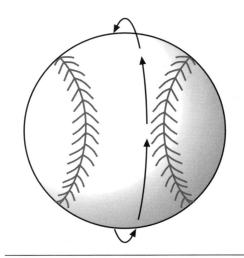

Figure 8.1 Correct backward spin of the rise ball.

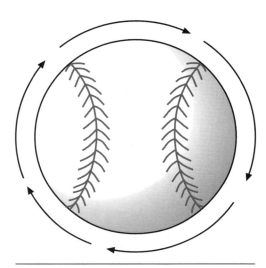

Figure 8.2 Vertical right-to-left spin.

or as high as the shoulder, but it must be on a straight path to the target until the ball is released.

The roll of the index finger again places the middle finger along a seam and rolls the index finger along the side of the ball. The two fingers (index and middle) are usually spread fairly far apart, placing some pressure on the knuckles of the index finger. At release, as the wrist snaps underneath the ball, the index finger should pinch toward the middle finger again, guiding the ball to leave the back of the hand.

The rise ball can be thrown with a two- or four-seam grip, depending on which seam the middle finger is on. There are arguments for better movement off both sets of seams. I recommend that pitchers master the techniques and spins and then experiment with both the two-seam and four-seam release. By observing the movement of the ball, the pitcher can determine which grip yields the best results for her.

a   b

Figure 8.3   Two common grips for the rise ball are *(a)* tucking or digging the index finger into the cover of the ball, and *(b)* rolling the index finger along the side.

Note that neither of the two grips is easy and comfortable. When learning the rise ball, the pitcher should spend a lot of time with a ball in her hand to become accustomed to the awkward feel and discomfort of the grips. She may have to toughen up her fingers by developing calluses. Throwing the rise ball generates a lot of friction on the index finger.

CUPPING AND COCKING

Two main techniques are used in snapping the wrist for the rise ball. In cupping the wrist (see figure 8.4), the pitcher does just that—she slightly cups the wrist when leaving the glove and approaches the snap from

Figure 8.4   Cupping the wrist.

underneath the ball. In cupping the ball, the pitcher simply slides underneath and past the ball at release.

The second technique is known as cocking the wrist (see figure 8.5). Unlike cupping, in which the wrist bends slightly inward, cocking bends the wrist back or outward and positions the hand behind or even on top of the ball when approaching the snap. At release, instead of simply sliding underneath the ball, the wrist makes a full snap to pass by and force the ball off the back of the hand.

RELEASE POINT

The release point of the rise ball must be on an upward angle. The lower a pitcher can start the rise on an upward angle, the more movement she

Figure 8.5   Cocking the wrist.

will have *through* the zone. Many factors play into how low a pitcher is able to start the pitch, but the bottom line is that she releases the ball on an upward path.

The pitcher must understand that she cannot throw the ball 60 miles per hour *against* the direction she wants it to break and expect the spin to overcome the force of the speed. In other words, she cannot throw a rise ball downward at 60 miles per hour and expect the spin to move it back upward. If she does not provide the angle to the pitch at release, it will become a flat rise ball and likely result in a solid hit.

POSTURE AND WEIGHT SHIFT

Body positioning will determine how low in the zone the pitch can begin and still have an upward angle. Exactly opposite the forward drop-ball posture, posture for the rise ball angles slightly backward. The hips should land and stay behind the stride leg, and the shoulders should land and stay behind the hips (see figure 8.6).

Use the following as a guide. With the fastball, the body drives *to* the stride leg. With the drop ball, the body drives *through* the stride leg. And with the rise ball, the body drives *against* the stride leg. Most of the body weight stays behind the pitch. The stride leg serves as a solid base, and the body must land behind that base and remain there throughout the pitch.

Figure 8.6 Compare the postures of the fastball, drop, and rise.

a   b

Figure 8.7 Because the rise ball posture is angled slightly backward, the weight will settle on the drive leg.

The back leg will continue to move forward through the pitch. But with the posture angled slightly backward, after the snap the drive leg will catch the weight of the body as the momentum lands behind the stride leg (see the sequence in figure 8.7).

Correct posture and weight shift allow the pitcher to begin the ball lower in the zone while giving the ball its necessary upward angle. In short, the pitcher can place upward angle on the ball either by the angle of the arm circle at release (see figure 8.8a) or by the angle of body positioning at release (see figure 8.8b). These two approaches will have different heights of release.

a   b

Figure 8.8 In (a), the pitcher has no posture or weight shift for the rise ball. Therefore, she must rely solely on the angle of her arm to start the pitch upward. In (b), the pitcher has set correct weight shift and posture which helps create the release of the upward angle from a much lower starting point.

Many pitchers have difficulty keeping the rise ball in the strike zone. If they release it high, they get good movement but the ball is always out of the zone. When they adjust the release to a lower point, the pitch flattens out and does not move. The cause of this problem is usually poor body positioning and perhaps the physical inability to hold the correct positioning. The answer is hard work and body awareness, not, as most people would like to believe, a simple lowering of the release point.

Another key factor in body positioning is the angle of the shoulders. As the stride foot lands, the body must land angled backward with the glove-side shoulder toward the catcher (see figure 8.9a). It is important with the rise ball that the glove-side shoulder must remain in front and slightly higher than the throwing-arm shoulder (see figure 8.9b). Although the throwing hand snaps underneath the ball, the throwing shoulder remains behind and slightly lower than the glove shoulder. This positioning is crucial. The natural tendency is for the throwing shoulder to rotate through. If this happens, the backward spin will be impossible to maintain. A simple rule of thumb is that the angle of the spin will match the angle of the shoulders. Keep an eye on the glove here. If the glove flies aggressively to the side, the shoulders will rotate prematurely.

a   b

Figure 8.9 At the land of the stride foot *(a)*, the glove-side shoulder is toward the catcher, and through release *(b)*, the shoulder remains in front and slightly higher than the throwing-arm shoulder.

DRILLS AND ROUTINES FOR THE RISE BALL

In learning the rise ball, the pitcher should work on some strengthening exercises. The stronger the forearm, the faster the wrist snaps; the faster the spin, the more severe the movement. Females do not have as much natural strength in their wrists and forearms as their male counterparts, so this pitch is more difficult to master.

If a pitcher decides to undertake the rise ball, she should keep a ball in her hand as much as possible—while sitting on the couch, talking on the phone, walking around the house, standing around the park. This routine will help the pitcher adapt to the awkward feeling of the grip and allow her to start spinning the ball to herself and understanding the path that the hand and fingers must take to impart the correct spin. After the path becomes a habit, the pitcher can work on snapping the wrist faster. Increasing the speed of the wrist snap is accomplished in the same way as increasing throwing speed— the more the pitcher snaps at her top speed, the more likely it is that she will increase that top speed. Following are some of my favorite drills to develop the rise ball.

PRACTICE IT ## Spinner Drill

The first step in learning the rise ball is mastering the backward spin. Using a Spinner is one of the most effective ways to see and understand the rotation and the movements required to cause it. Pitchers and even coaches sometimes cannot see the spin of the ball. The flat Spinner reveals the rotation.

The pitcher should start by spinning the Spinner backward to herself. She may find this feat awkward and difficult at first. After the pitcher can smoothly spin the ball backward, she can begin to rock back and toss to a catcher or wall four or five feet away (see figure 8.10). The pitcher will have to concentrate on straight follow-through and quick movements during release. Each time she accomplishes the spin, she can move back couple of feet. I recommend going at least three-quarters of the distance without using the circle. When the pitcher feels confident enough to add the circle, she should come

Figure 8.10 The pitcher rocks back and tosses the Spinner to the catcher.

back up to the four- or five-foot range again and work backward. She should throw the Spinner at full distance and full speed before adding the ball. When adding the ball, she starts close again.

PRACTICE IT

Oversized and Undersized Ball Spins

Using a baseball or an 11-inch ball may help the pitcher make the correct movements to get underneath the ball. The smaller size of the ball allows the fingers to be more flexible and allows the correct movements to occur with less effort. A pitcher can use an undersized ball when initially trying to create muscle memory for the correct spin movements.

An oversized ball is helpful in speeding up the wrist snap because the hand must pass under more area in the same amount of time. The oversized ball can also illustrate the spin to a pitcher who may be struggling with the backward concept. A 14-inch ball seems to be the perfect size because the pitcher can hold on to it comfortably throughout the circle before snapping the wrist at release. The routine used with these balls can mirror the routine used with the Spinner—starting close up without the circle and adding distance as well as the full circle.

PRACTICE IT

One-Knee Drill

The one-knee drill places the pitcher on her drive-leg knee with the stride leg extended out in front. The pitcher should not put much weight, if any, on the stride leg because this would shift her weight forward. Remember, in throwing the rise ball, the weight stays behind the stride leg. Because the pitcher is positioned on her knees, the lower body remains stationary, allowing her to work on upper-body mechanics, such as shoulder positioning and posture, in an isolated environment. The pitcher should start with a catcher approximately 10 feet away and progress to full distance.

PRACTICE IT

Flat Spins

The mere mention of flat spins will make most pitchers and even some coaches cringe. The flat-spin drill, however, is one of my favorites. Many pitchers can spin the ball backward only when they release the ball high. This is because, the higher they release the ball, the more time they have to pass underneath it before release.

In doing flat spins, the goal is to release the ball at about knee height. For this drill only, the pitcher need not worry much about the upward angle. Releasing the ball at knee height will force the pitcher to start and finish the spin much more quickly than she does when releasing at shoulder or head height. If a pitcher can master a backward spin at knee height, the spin will be a piece of cake when she adds the angle of release to the formula and starts the ball slightly higher.

Most pitchers make a mistake by practicing the rise spins to higher targets (usually with the catcher standing) and then trying to work their way down. The pitch just keeps becoming more challenging and difficult because she must finish the release quicker and quicker. But if the pitcher practices at the quickest release point most of the time, anything beyond that will seem easy!

PRACTICE IT

Rope Drill

The rope drill for the rise ball is similar to the rope drill with the change-up. The rope should be approximately 7 to 10 feet in front of home plate, stomach high to the hitter, or three to four feet off the ground (see figure 8.11). The goal is for the pitch to pass underneath the rope and finish above it. The pitch that does this has the correct movement. For variation, the rope can be placed at the halfway point to show where the pitch is when the hitter is deciding whether to swing or not. For this drill, catchers should hold the ball for a second so that the pitcher can see if the ball rose above the rope or not.

I recommend that catchers remain in the down position when working with pitchers on rise balls. Many catchers automatically stand to catch the rise-ball spins, encouraging the pitcher to throw the ball high. It is OK for the catcher to start by catching a few pitches in the standing position, but she should do most of the workout in a squat position or in a seated position (for the dad catchers!).

Figure 8.11 The rope is placed 7 to 10 feet in front of home plate, 3 to 4 feet off the ground.

Spinning or positioning drills often become part of a pitcher's pregame warm-up. I think this is a smart idea. The more effort that goes into getting things right in the warm-up, the better the expectations can be for the performance.

THE FINAL PITCH

In teaching lessons, camps, and clinics, I find that parents are always eager for their children to learn how to throw the rise ball. But the athlete must have the same enthusiasm because the rise ball requires lots of hard work and a focused body and mind. In addition, the pitcher must have a certain amount of strength and pitch speed for the pitch to even have a chance to work.

As always, fundamental mistakes will be magnified when approaching the rise ball. If a pitcher does not have a good power-line stride, glove positioning, or balance, throwing the spin will be impossible. If the pitcher is unable to steer with the stride leg, placement of the pitch inside or outside will compromise its effectiveness. Learning the rise ball is difficult enough without having to relearn fundamental mechanics along the way.

CURVEBALL

The curveball is a popular pitch for female pitchers. The curve is most effective when it passes through and out of the strike zone, but it can also be successful when it moves into the zone. The goal of the pitcher when moving the ball out of the zone is to run the pitch out of reach of the hitter (see figure 9.1a). When moving the ball into the zone, the goal is to fool the hitter into taking a pitch she believes to be a ball (see figure 9.1b).

The downside of the curve is the fact that it does not change vertical planes suddenly or unpredictably, making it easier for the hitter to track and contact solidly. A good pitcher can work the curveball up and down, but the height movement will be secondary and subtle.

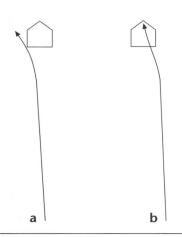

Figure 9.1 A curveball *(a)* breaking out of the zone and *(b)* breaking into the zone.

CHARACTERISTICS AND EXPECTATIONS

The curveball will move sideways from right to left for a right-handed pitcher and left to right for a left-handed pitcher. As mentioned earlier, the curve can be thrown low or high, but the primary movement will still be sideways, or horizontal. The ball should be released on a slight angle toward the target, providing a positive environment for the spin. If the pitcher throws the curve against the direction she intends it to break, the movement will be stifled.

The more severe the angle of the pitch, the more severe the break can become. For this reason, a right-handed pitcher will gain much more break on a curve that starts on the inside half of the plate and moves across and off the outside corner than she would on a curve that starts off the plate to the inside and comes to the inside corner. The angles across the zone are better.

One of the most difficult aspects of the curveball is gaining a flat horizontal spin rather than a vertical spin. A vertically spinning ball (see figure 9.2a) can move across the zone aggressively, but the flat horizontal spin (see figure 9.2b) will cause the ball to move more suddenly. To accomplish the horizontal spin, the fingers must move *around* the ball instead of passing sideways underneath the ball (see figure 9.3).

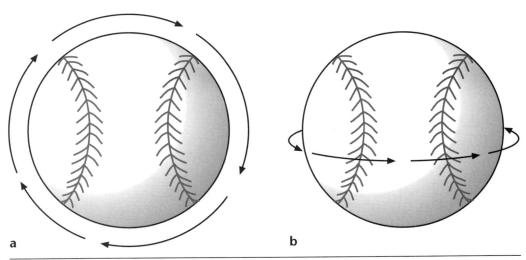

a   b

Figure 9.2 With a curveball, you're not going for *(a)* vertical spin, but instead *(b)* horizontal spin.

a   b

Figure 9.3 To accomplish a horizontal spin, the fingers move *(a)* around the ball instead of *(b)* sideways underneath the ball.

GRIPS

Grips and wrist-snapping techniques for the curve are similar to those used for the rise ball. Many pitchers still tuck or roll the index finger while placing the middle finger along a seam for a two- or four-seam rotation. Pitchers can experiment with cupping or cocking the wrist, grips, and two- or four-seam rotations to see which techniques yield the best results.

Although some pitchers choose to roll or dig the index finger as they do with the rise, many choose to leave the index finger lying flat. The index finger laid flat on the ball should be located along a seam to achieve as much torque as possible at release. The key here is to find something comfortable that also develops maximum spin speed.

As mentioned at the outset of the book, the thumb should always be located on a seam. With the curveball, however, it is sometimes helpful to locate the thumb on a seam that is closer to the index finger as opposed to around the ball more. Some pitchers prefer to keep the thumb closer to the index finger, feeling that doing so makes the wrist snap around the ball more easily and more naturally.

POSTURE AND WEIGHT SHIFT

The posture for the curveball should tilt slightly in the direction of the desired movement. The pitcher leans slightly toward her glove side at stride-foot contact (see figure 9.4). As she releases the pitch, her body falls in the direction of the lean. Many pitchers tend to twist the torso at release, causing the ball to have an extreme angle out of the zone. The hand should lead the pitch through, and the body follows.

Another detail that will help the point of release and ultimately the angle of the pitch is the positioning of the stride foot. The stride foot should cross over the drive leg and land slightly across the power line. This positioning will allow the pitch to start farther over and maximize movement with the angle of release. It is helpful

Figure 9.4 At stride-foot land, the pitcher will lean slightly toward the glove side.

to position the stride foot even or in line with the intended starting target (see figure 9.5). For instance, if the pitcher wants the pitch to start off the inside corner of the plate and move into the zone, she should place the stride foot even with the inside starting location. This will allow the ball, which starts to the side of the stride, to be released on an angle toward its target.

DRILLS AND ROUTINES FOR THE CURVEBALL

Although the technical movements of the spin differ, the rise and curve are similar in many ways. Therefore, many of the drills used with the rise are effective with the curve as well. Spinners and over- and undersized balls are great ways to learn, polish, and speed up the spin of the curveball. A few of the other drills include slight variations.

PRACTICE IT
Two-Knees Drill

In contrast to the one-knee drill used for the rise, in this drill the pitcher places both knees on the ground and angles them at 45 degrees to home plate (see figure 9.6). She starts with no circle and works spins with a catcher about 10 feet away. As the techniques become habit, she adds the circle and gradually backs up the catcher to three-quarters distance.

PRACTICE IT
Rope or Noodle Drill

Some coaches like to hang a rope or string from the ceiling for this one. I like to use a swimmer's noodle anchored by a large coupling, but either will do. The noodle or rope should be five to seven feet in front of home plate and widthwise where

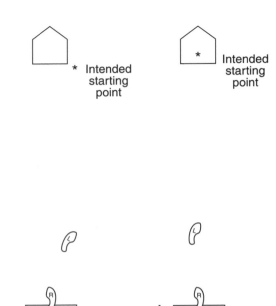

Figure 9.5 Position the stride foot at least even with the intended starting point of the ball: *(a)* step in line with starting point off the plate to start ball off the plate inside; *(b)* step directly to the middle to start ball in middle of plate and break across.

Figure 9.6 Positioning for the two-knees drill.

the pitcher or coach would like the ball to be when it reaches that location. The pitcher breaks the ball around the noodle (see figure 9.7). A right-handed pitcher will pass the noodle on the right side and, if the ball breaks effectively, she will see the pitch caught on the other side of the noodle. This drill is also an effective way to practice stride-foot placement. The pitcher should be striding across the power line and to the throwing-arm side of the noodle, since this is where it is intended for the ball to start.

Figure 9.7   A left-handed pitch passes the noodle on the left (and a right-handed pitch passes on the right). If the ball breaks effectively, the left-handed pitcher will see the pitch caught on the other side of the noodle.

As with the pitcher who wants to throw the rise ball, the prospective curveball pitcher should enhance her capability by increasing the strength of her wrists and forearms. Greater strength will allow her to snap more quickly and spin the ball faster, yielding more severe movement.

THE FINAL PITCH

The curveball can be an effective pitch in a pitcher's arsenal and can also be a dominant pitch for some pitchers. After mastering rotation, the pitcher can make the pitch more versatile by working on throwing the pitch low and high as well as "stair stepping" through and out of the zone with sequential pitches. This will put a different look and location on the pitch and prevent it from becoming predictable.

I do not recommend learning a curve and rise ball at the same time. The pitcher should focus on one or the other until one of the spins becomes habit before mixing the two. The reason for this is that the hand movement for correct spin on the curve moves across and around the ball and the follow-through crosses the body. That very movement will cause the pitcher to make a mistake with the rise spin time and time again. Therefore, in large part, the proper technique for the curveball cultivates incorrect muscle memory for the rise. After the pitcher learns one or the other, however, learning the new pitch and movements can be easier.

SCREWBALL

The screwball has recently become more popular with females in fastpitch softball. Although it is a go-to pitch for some pitchers, it plays a much better role in the arsenal as a lower percentage mix pitch. Because of the underhand motion passing by the hip, it is physically impossible to get correct directional spin and angle on the screwball and stay legally within the limitations of pitching. Thus the screwball moves more gradually than other movement pitches. The severe cuts and jumps that you may see on the rise, drop, and curve are more subtle with the screwball.

Many pitchers like to use the screwball as a mixing pitch that will stay tight on the inside of the hitter's zone. As the ball moves in or away, the hitter often has a difficult read to determine how tight the ball will finish on or off the corners. Pitchers commonly use the screwball with high and low targets rather than staying in the middle of the zone. Pitchers who throw lots of curves like to show batters the opposite placement by complementing them with the screwball.

CHARACTERISTICS AND EXPECTATIONS

The movement of the screwball is directly opposite the movement of the curveball. For a right-handed pitcher, the curve breaks from right to left, or *away* from the pitching arm. Conversely, for a right-handed pitcher, the screwball breaks from left to right, or *toward* the pitching arm (see figure 10.1).

Figure 10.1 The curveball breaks away from the pitching arm; the screwball breaks toward the pitching arm (this diagram reflects a right-handed pitcher).

As mentioned earlier, the screwball is most effective when thrown from the middle of the plate toward or off the corner. The pitcher's goal is to tuck this pitch in tight on the handle of the bat (for a right-handed pitcher to right-handed hitter), as shown in figure 10.2a, or run it out of the zone and out of reach of the hitter (right-handed pitcher to left-handed hitter), as shown in figure 10.2b. Like the curve, the screwball is more effective with a greater angle of release.

GRIPS AND RELEASES

The grip of the screwball can vary from method to method and with personal preference for two or four seams. Most pitchers choose to leave the index finger lying flat along a seam rather than curled or tucked. The pitcher can choose either of two methods to snap the wrist and impart spin for the screwball.

The first method allows a straight-off release and imparts downward spin on the ball, just like the action on a peel drop or fastball. The pitcher uses the horseshoe grip as detailed in chapter 1 for the fastball (see figure 10.3). The ball will again roll directly off the fingertips. The pitcher should try putting a *little* extra pressure on the index and middle fingers to give the ball a slight tilt.

With this type of release on the screwball, the pitcher relies on the nature of the ball itself. The long seams moving through the air provide a slight break inward for the screw. The amount of movement will vary from brand to brand and sometimes even from ball to ball.

Figure 10.2 Here, a right-handed pitcher aims the screwball *(a)* in on a right-handed hitter, and *(b)* out on a left-handed hitter.

Figure 10.3 The horseshoe grip.

The second grip places the index finger or middle finger along a seam. The fingers can be placed along the close seams for a two-seam rotation or along the wide seams for a four-seam rotation (see figure 10.4). At release, the

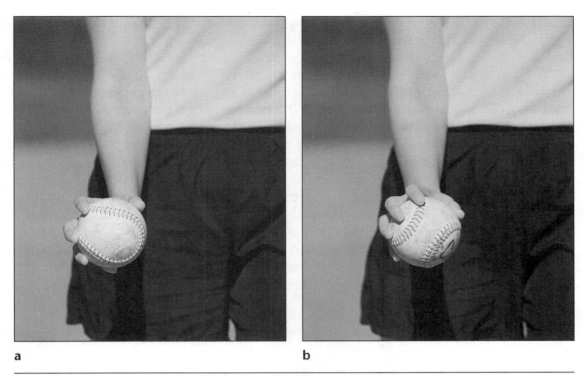

a   b

Figure 10.4 Placing the index finger *(a)* on the close seams for a two-seam rotation, or *(b)* on the wide seams for a four-seam rotation.

pitcher twists the ball and allows it to leave off the side of the index finger, causing a vertically spinning rotation (clockwise for a right-handed pitcher and opposite for a left-handed pitcher) and a fade or slight break inward when released at the proper angle (see figure 10.5). This particular release is the common mistake that pitchers make when throwing the rise and curve. So, due to muscle memory and the tendency of habit, a pitcher who throws a lot of screwballs may find learning the rise and curve a little more difficult.

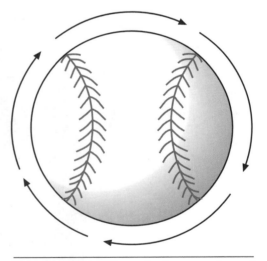

Figure 10.5 The spinning rotation of the ball.

POSTURE AND WEIGHT SHIFT

The primary goal in throwing the screwball is to release the ball on the correct angle. The stride land will be crucial in accomplishing this. If stride-foot placement is in the middle or across the power line, the starting point of the pitch will already be toward the inside corner of the plate (see figure 10.6).

Because that is the direction of desired movement, the only place for movement is out of the zone.

For that reason the stride leg must land on the glove-arm side of the power line (right-handed pitchers land left of the line and left-handed pitchers land right of the line). This stride-leg placement allows movement horizontally across the entire zone. When movement is maximized across the zone, pitch location becomes more difficult for the hitter to anticipate.

Once the stride leg lands, the trunk and lower body should be positioned over the foot with the head leaning slightly toward the direction of desired movement (see figure 10.7). After release, the body will follow through and land in the direction of the pitch. A common mistake for pitchers throwing the screwball is the failure to balance and hold the position until *after* releasing the ball. They stride off to the side correctly but immediately lose their balance and fall during the pitch. This action will push the release of the ball farther toward the break and will either minimize the angle of movement or push the pitch severely out of the zone.

Figure 10.6 Stepping inside or toward the middle limits the effectiveness of the screwball. To prevent starting the pitch too far inside, keep the ball snug to the hip.

Figure 10.7 Correct position at release. The step to the far glove side of the right-handed pitcher allows for maximum movement across the zone.

DRILLS AND ROUTINES FOR THE SCREWBALL

In learning the screwball the pitcher must be aware of its effect on muscle memory and the result it may have on the correct movements of the rise and curve. I would recommend establishing one of the other two pitches before beginning to learn the screwball. Gaining spin for the screwball is relatively easy and will not take a great deal of technique work, but the pitcher should focus on spinning the ball as quickly as possible.

Drills for the screwball can be copied from the previous pitches. The pitcher can use the Spinner and over- and undersized balls to work on the correct spin and the speed of spin. The larger ball can sometimes help with the perception of correct movement, and the smaller ball can help develop the physical ability to release the ball correctly off the side of the hand. The Spinner can reveal both spins so that the pitcher can check if they are correct. The spin can often be difficult to see with balls.

PRACTICE IT The noodle or string placed vertically (as with the curveball) in front of the catcher provides a target around which the pitcher can move the ball, using movement opposite the curveball movement. If the pitcher can throw the curve, an enjoyable addition to this drill is to place the noodle about 10 to 15 feet in front of home plate and in the middle of the plate widthwise. Alternating between the curve and the screwball, the pitcher tries to throw each pitch around the noodle (see figure 10.8). The curve (for a right-handed pitcher) will travel around the right side of the noodle, and the screw will travel around the left side of the noodle. The catcher should freeze the ball for a few seconds to show the severity of the movement.

PRACTICE IT Another drill that is helpful in mastering the positions, balance, and release path of the arm is the one-leg drill. As with the one-leg drill for the drop ball, the pitcher takes her position with the stride leg already in place. The location of the stride should be to the glove side of the middle power line. The back leg should be dangling with the toe touching for balance. The head should be set slightly toward the throwing-arm side, causing the posture to be slightly tilted. This position is known as a controlled off-balance position.

From this position, the pitcher should make the circle (50 to 75 percent of full speed) and release the ball. After release, she will fall toward the throwing-arm side. This drill places the body in the correct landing position. The pitcher can feel that position and perform the movements required to complete the pitch. The noodle can be added to the one-leg drill after the pitcher is comfortable with the standard drill.

Maximizing the angle for the pitch path is the key to obtaining the greatest possible deception without sharp movement. Here are some key points to watch for in trying to maximize angles:

- The pitcher must stride correctly to her glove side of the middle power line. Some pitchers are unaware of stride-foot location and focus only on spinning or leaning. If the stride foot does not position itself on the outer edge, the pitch does not have a chance from the start.

a   b

Figure 10.8 Notice the left-handed pitcher *(a)* goes around the noodle with a curveball. To get the same directional movement, the right-handed pitcher *(b)* must use the screwball. Notice how clearly the noodle shows the placement of the pitches.

- Balance must be over the stride leg until the pitch is released. Many pitchers immediately fall to the side when their weight moves to the stride leg. They must master the hang time over the front leg until they release the ball.

- The pitcher should keep the release point and path of the arm close to the stride leg. Failing to do this is probably the most common mistake pitchers make with the screwball. After the stride foot is set and the body is balancing in position, the arm and hand must pass closely by the stride leg.

- The pitcher must stay legal. In learning the screwball, pitchers often get carried away with the sideways stride. The stride foot must land *inside* the imaginary 24-inch lines that extend off each side of the rubber. The goal is to maximize the angle without flirting with an illegal pitch.

THE FINAL PITCH

I hesitate to teach the screwball to younger pitchers and introduce it only after the pitcher has mastered fundamental techniques. Even then, I encourage its use only as an occasional mix pitch. Coaches and pitchers must realize that the techniques of the screwball, such as its stride location, sideways release, and off-balance finish to the throwing-hand side, are mistakes in throwing the fastball, mistakes that young pitchers often work diligently to overcome. Repeated too often, these movements will bleed into other pitches and destroy mechanics.

For the most part, the screwball should be used as an enhancement pitch and mixed into the pitcher's arsenal. A dominant pitch should have a more severe cut and better movement. Used correctly, however, the screwball can be very effective in complicating a hitter's at bat by attacking the corner of the plate or zone with an angle more aggressive than that of the straight fastball.

PART III

FIVE MORE FACTORS FOR EXCELLENT PITCHING

In watching a softball game most people notice the obvious physical characteristics of an elusive pitch, great play, stolen base, or home run. Trained athletes, however, know that much goes into the setup, strategy, and positioning that precedes a great pitch, catch, hit, or play. These are the intangibles—the factors often overlooked by the ordinary spectator.

For 10 years, I played Women's Major level softball against the most successful dynasty of the sport—the Raybestos Brakettes. And during that time, they were in the finals of the National Tournament every year, winning it more times than not.

I used to look at the team of veteran players from all across the country and wonder how, year after year, they continued their dominance over the talented and usually younger rosters of the nation's top competitors. Sure, the Brakettes were made up of the best of the best, but the country had more than 12 top players. The dominance of the Brakettes was obvious, and their consistency never failed.

The answer I was looking for was not on the outside, but on the inside. In 1991, I was fortunate enough to find out firsthand. After a lifetime of watching and playing against them, I was asked to play with the Brakettes. The secret to their success was, in the words of Ralph Raymond, "the little things." Everyone we played could catch and throw and pitch and hit, but could they communicate with each other to be precise when it mattered most, funnel nervousness into positive energy, stay focused on a common goal throughout the season, always be prepared, and work as one to accomplish the goal?

What I learned from my experience on the Brakettes was professionalism. Not in the sense of a paycheck (which is the extent of many definitions), but in the sense of an attitude and a way of life. In an environment where team practices were few and far between, each player remained at the top of her game by taking responsibility for herself and her abilities. Individuals practiced together or on their own on off days, and prepared themselves to play on game days without every move being choreographed by a coach or trainer. Each player knew her role in the team's success and showed up prepared to play her best at games. Each individual approached the game with a level of seriousness about her job.

To excel at something, it has to be a part of your everyday life. Physical conditioning, mental thought processes and focus, practice routines and techniques, and developing a relationship with your catcher are all extra things that you do as a pitcher to reach your potential. These intangibles are factors that are not accomplished solely by attending a team practice.

Pitchers have an above-average responsibility on the outcome of the game, and it takes an above-average commitment to fulfill that responsibility. It takes a willingness to go the extra mile and to attempt to gain every possible advantage. Realize that the advantages are not always obvious. That, however, does not make them any less effective.

Challenge yourself with the issues of the following chapters. Some of you may already be establishing and gaining from the intangibles. But it is crucial that you identify, recognize, and train for these elements, right alongside the more obvious and tangible fundamentals. In the end, it takes the complete package to succeed.

CATCHER

11

The greatest asset of any pitcher is the person squatting in front of her. The catcher has an enormous effect on the performance of the pitcher. A good catcher allows a pitcher to have confidence and frees her to focus on the job of executing each pitch. The spotlight often focuses on the pitcher's circle, but the teamwork of the pitcher and catcher is ultimately the key to a successful performance.

SHARING THE COMMON GOAL

In an average seven-inning game the pitcher throws between 80 and 100 pitches. Executing each one with precision is not easy. To perform at her best, the pitcher must be able to concentrate on the present pitch.

The pitcher will have greater focus and confidence when:

- she knows that the pitch will be caught;
- she is able to throw the pitch appropriate for the situation because the catcher can handle the ball in the dirt (as with the drop), can move quickly enough to track the movement (as with the rise or curve), doesn't mind being shaken off, and is generally adaptable to the situation;
- she has the authority to shake off a pitch;
- the catcher uses a good solid catch and frame instead of a loose glove;
- the catcher works positively with the umpire; and
- the catcher displays a visible sense of confidence.

We established the importance of the catcher and the effect she will ultimately have on the performance, so the catcher must take an equal share in the performance of the pitcher—good or bad. As mentioned in previous chapters, the pitcher's goals are (primary) to strike out the hitter and (secondary) to control the hitter. The catcher should share those goals, and she has the best chance of achieving them with a pitcher who is confident and focused.

KNOWING THE PITCHER

The catcher must know her pitcher. She must know the pitcher's emotional makeup—how the pitcher thinks, what bothers her, and what motivates her. The catcher must know when the pitcher is nervous, when she is distracted, when she is on or off, and what she is comfortable with as a routine. The catcher must know the pitcher's physical capabilities—what pitches she has mastered and can use effectively, what her go-to pitch is, which pitches are working today, how strong she is, and what her stamina level is. The catcher should know the pitcher's percentages of accuracy and execution on targets and movement pitches, and perhaps know some focus or trigger points that can help the pitcher when she struggles with a certain target or pitch.

Whether the previously mentioned factors are strengths or weaknesses depends on the perception and awareness of the catcher. When the pitcher is trying to get ahead of the hitter and throw a first-pitch strike, the catcher should call a pitch that she *knows* the pitcher is likely to throw for a strike. If the catcher calls a low-percentage first pitch to every hitter, she will constantly put her pitcher behind in the count. Pitch calling is equally important later in the count. If the pitcher is in a good situation to strike out the hitter, the catcher should call for a pitch that she believes will beat the hitter, instead of just randomly calling pitches.

On the emotional side of things, if the catcher is aware that the pitcher is having trouble focusing on a certain day, she can do something to remedy the situation. She may want to slow the pitcher's pace, talk to her between innings, or offer reassurance through body language, gestures, or verbal encouragement. If the catcher recognizes that the pitcher is throwing more balls far out of the zone than normal, she may surmise that the pitcher is trying too hard to throw the ball by the hitters, is intimidated by the hitters, or is attempting to force the movement. She can address such possibilities directly or indirectly with the pitcher and possibly solve the problem before it gets out of hand.

A mistake commonly made by both coaches and catchers is believing that all pitches of a given type are equal. If a particular team or hitter does not do well against the rise ball, the coach and catcher may believe that to be true with *any* rise ball. Write this down—all rise balls are not equal. The same goes for any pitch. The catcher should evaluate the effectiveness of each pitcher and call the game based on who is on the mound and what pitches are her particular strengths.

KNOWING THE HITTERS

After establishing the strengths and weaknesses of the pitcher, the catcher can contribute to the goals by learning the hitters. All hitters have weaknesses—in the stance, swing, count, focus, or other areas. If the catcher takes on the task of finding and exposing those weaknesses, the pitcher will be able to concentrate solely on executing each pitch.

Good pitchers will tell you that they enjoy nothing more than being able to focus on throwing the pitches that are called. Some pitchers do not have that luxury. If a catcher is not conscious of the hitter's strengths and weaknesses and does not accept the challenge of doing the thinking, then that responsibility falls back on the pitcher. With strategizing clouding up her focus, the pitcher may compromise her pitch execution. The pitcher should work with the catcher when necessary so that both have a solid understanding of what the other is thinking.

In analyzing strengths and weaknesses of a hitter, the catcher must keep in mind the strengths and weaknesses of the pitcher.

A good relationship between the pitcher and the catcher is crucial to their interaction and success.

In the strategy of pitch calling, the catcher should use all available information. For instance, a pitcher's strength may outweigh a hitter's strength. For example, a hitter who likes a low outside pitch may be a strikeout to a pitcher with a good drop on the outside corner. Just because a hitter loves to hit a particular pitch does not mean that it would be a poor one to call and throw, especially if the pitch is the strength of the pitcher.

PHYSICAL ATTRIBUTES

The physical skills of a catcher can directly affect the performance of a pitcher. One of the physical skills of the catcher is framing the pitch. A good catcher will catch the ball solidly and hold the ball still. To frame the pitch, the catcher moves smoothly and catches the ball in a way that may give the umpire a more favorable opinion of the location. Umpires come to depend on and trust good catchers, and they sometimes give the location of the glove a second look. That second look will often make a borderline pitch a called strike.

Catchers who are not skilled in the art of framing may have a sloppy glove (one that does not stay still when catching the pitch) or, even worse, have a tendency to yank and pull the ball into the strike zone. A sloppy glove allows the impact of a pitch on the edge to carry the ball out of the zone and make it no longer appear to be a strike. The yanking or pulling of the glove not only insults the umpire but on a borderline pitch gives the impression that the catcher did not believe it was enough of a strike to leave it still. Either way, the umpire will probably call the borderline pitch a ball.

The catcher can also hinder the pitcher by not moving forward and backward according to the hitter's location in the batter's box. Remember that the catcher must throw the pitch to move before the hitter. In the case of a drop ball, if the hitter moves to the front of the box and the catcher stays back, all the drops will hit the dirt before they reach the catcher. This oversight on the part of the catcher could render the drop ball useless against a particular hitter or during an entire game. What if the drop is that pitcher's best pitch?

Another physical technique that can cause problems is the catcher automatically standing up when the ball is in the upper part of the zone. The proper technique is to reach as high as possible with the arm before extending the legs. Some catchers begin to stand up before they have reached. This action blocks the vision of the umpire and gives an indication that the pitch is too high when it may not be.

FINDING AND DEVELOPING A GOOD CATCHER

Once the pitcher realizes the importance of a good catcher, the next question is how to get one. First, the pitcher should find someone who enjoys the position, likes the challenge of meeting the physical and mental demands, and does not mind working hard in practice and games. The pitcher and catcher will spend many hours together to develop and perfect throwing and catching the pitches.

Many pitchers have devoted parents who want to catch for them and love to do it. But I always tell my pitchers that no competitive situation will allow their dads or moms to squat behind the plate and catch the game for them. So although this situation may be fun for both athlete and parent, the pitcher should spend the majority of her practice time working with a real catcher so that the two of them can learn the many aspects of calling, pitching, catching, and executing the pitches.

Practicing Together

In the ideal situation, the pitcher and catcher always know what the other is thinking. They both understand the call and the shakeoff, have mutual respect for the tough job involved in the other's position, and never have a conflict. Of course, we do not usually have the perfect scenario, at least not at first. That is why spending time practicing together is so important. The two can develop considerably by practicing at times without a parent or coach breathing down their necks. Open discussion of what is happening can then take place without overwhelming control by a coach or parent. The players should let the relationship build gradually through an understanding of mutual goals.

Although the on-field relationship is crucial, the pitcher and catcher need not be best friends off the field. I have seen and experienced many situations in which the pitcher and catcher had little in common besides softball. This is not a problem. As long as the on-field relationship is cohesive and professional, the players can accomplish the ultimate goal. Personal feelings and friendships should not interfere with any aspect of the game on the field or "between the lines."

In rare situations, pitchers have come to me about catchers who are difficult to get along with and stubborn in their ways of calling or catching. Even so, I recommend that the pitcher and catcher practice together to work most of this out. Sometimes a pitcher and her parent or coach will overwhelm a catcher with demands shortly before competition without taking time to explain. The catcher, not understanding the requests, tends to do what comes naturally instead of experimenting with a lot of new ideas that do not make much sense to her. This sort of conflict can often be alleviated if the catcher has spent time practicing regularly with the pitcher during lessons and practices.

Catchers can benefit from professional coaching for their particular position. They often find it easier to hear corrections from someone who they believe has their best interest in mind.

Working on Skills

As mentioned before, working together in practices can go a long way toward building a positive relationship. Practices are also a great time for the catcher to work on her particular skills. For instance, for drop balls she should move up on the plate slightly. Knowing that the balls are mostly going downward, she can anticipate and practice framing the low one that stays out of the dirt, picking up the short hop, and blocking the longer ones. On rise balls, the catcher can practice staying down and reaching up for the ball with full arm extension before using the legs. Catching fastballs is a favorable time to practice maintaining a strong glove position and not allowing pitches to move the hand. Catchers often make mistakes in games simply because they lack experience. Practice with a pitcher is the perfect way to practice the normal techniques hundreds of times.

Speed drills, discussed earlier in the book, are an excellent way for the pitcher and catcher to work together in competition against the clock or against other pitchers and catchers. In testing themselves for times or in races, both pitcher and catcher will be working on quickness. We also discussed the distance drill, with the pitcher backing up and throwing distances to check mechanics. Because catchers are often required to throw over 84 feet with accuracy, they too can use this drill to work on distance throwing. One other tip: sometime during or after practice, the pitcher should offer to catch some throws to second base for the catcher. The pitcher and catcher should both leave practice feeling satisfied that they are working on their own skills as well as helping each other develop.

A good catcher can enhance the performance of a pitcher in many ways. Unfortunately, the untrained spectator often fails to notice the catcher's contribution to the performance of the pitcher. But ask any great pitcher how much it matters to her to have a great catcher and then sit back and listen!

PRACTICE ROUTINES AND GAME PREPARATION

12

I never was miserable when I had a ball in my hand. We often talk about the hard work involved in being a good pitcher, but when I think back on my development, none of it ever seemed hard or like work. I enjoyed the challenges the hitters presented, and I enjoyed myself when I was pitching, whether that was in a practice or a game situation. On the other hand, I hated dance lessons, I hated practicing, and I hated dancing, period. I never was too good at dancing because it didn't matter to me. I didn't feel comfortable with it, and dancing was never much fun.

I think that sort of sums it up when you look at a pitcher's attitude toward practice. The desire to improve or spend time with pitching will be evident to a coach or parent, and it is a good indication of the seriousness of the athlete. Pitching takes time and patience if the athlete wants to excel. There is just no getting around it.

COMMITMENT TO A PRACTICE ROUTINE

One of the most important aspects to accomplishing anything is to have a routine. Pitching requires precision and speed, with location as well as movement. We established early on that being consistent with all of that would not be easy. So although repetition is necessary, it need not be grueling or miserable.

I mentioned earlier that the pitcher relaxing at home might hold a ball in her hand to become accustomed to grips. She might do short self-tosses to improve spin angles or spin speed. This sort of activity is not really an inconvenience. It is simply something that should cross the mind of a motivated pitcher and inspire her to pick up a ball.

Many parents worry about pushing their daughters too much. That concern is certainly one that bears discussion. If parents find themselves constantly reminding a child to practice, and from there it escalates into begging, bribing, or threatening, the parents may be in a negative situation with an athlete who has no desire to improve. The parent should take a closer look and ask the pitcher what her goals are. Does she just want to be with the rest of the kids and play a little ball along the way, or does she have aspirations for a future as a successful pitcher? Young people sometimes do not understand that to be good at *anything* requires dedication and commitment.

One thing that I believe sends mixed signals is a simple lack of organization. Although I do not believe that a parent should constantly force a pitcher to practice, I do believe that a parent should sit down and help the pitcher structure her time so that she can fit into a schedule the things that are important to her. The parent and child should look at the days of the week that will be good practice days and establish them as such.

For instance, the parent might say, "On Tuesdays, you get out of school early. Why don't you stay at the gym with Kelly and practice pitching for 45 minutes and I will pick you up after that? On Thursdays, your brother can catch for you in the backyard when you get home from school, and on Saturdays we can practice together in my warehouse at work." That sort of schedule is an organized practice week.

Between those three dates with a catcher, the pitcher can spend some time throwing into a net for a short time or work on spins, wrist snaps, or grips. Now that the pitcher has a set structure, she can fit in her other activities and accomplish more with her time. Many pitchers want to practice or don't mind practicing but just never get it organized.

THE CATCHING PARENT AND THE COACHING PARENT

One of the most difficult roles to master is being both a parent and a catcher or coach. By handling the situation correctly, however, the parent and child can lessen or even eliminate friction, disappointment, frustration, and hurt feelings. To accomplish that, both parties, the parent and the athlete, must relinquish their relationship as parent and daughter for the time that they are working together.

Some of my students contradict or challenge their parents with statements that they would never dream of saying to me. Because they are familiar with their parents, they do not demonstrate the same consideration and effort that they would to me. Athletes tend to argue with their parents and may even be combative at times. Establishing the parent as the coach, or even as someone who is giving unbiased feedback, will eliminate most of those problems.

On the other hand, I see parents say things to their daughters or respond to them in ways that they wouldn't consider doing with any other athlete.

Parents often seem to set higher standards for their own children and at times expect the impossible. If what a parent is expecting is unattainable, no one will be happy or satisfied. The parent will be creating a no-win situation.

Avoiding these pitfalls is not easy. The parent and athlete must try to be professional in their relationship during practices and games and offer the same consideration and courtesy to each other that they would to teammates, coaches, and other players. Most important, the parent and athlete must set boundaries that permit the relationship to revert to one of parent and daughter after the practice or game. Both parties need a release from analysis.

PRACTICE LOADS AND FREQUENCY

How often should a pitcher practice? How many pitches should she throw in a given workout? Pitchers and parents often ask these questions. Youth-level pitchers should try to practice a minimum of three times a week. Practice length should be relatively short so that boredom does not overwhelm focus. No matter what the length of the practice, it should end when the pitcher loses focus. If the pitcher is not concentrating on forming correct habits, chances are that she is repeating incorrect movements, thus ingraining them deeper as bad habits.

Practices on the youth level can be as simple as striding and driving on a power line for three sets of 10, performing towel drills, or doing wrist snaps. All these practices can be wrapped up in less than 15 minutes, and none involve pitching a ball to a catcher. My pitchers often give me the excuse that they did not have a catcher or a good environment in which to practice. If a pitcher is dedicated, she does not need the perfect situation. Many different ways of practicing are available. If space is limited, the pitcher can pitch into a net. At least once a week, however, the pitcher should try to find a spot to pitch to a catcher and work on putting it all together.

As a pitcher matures and begins to look at softball at the junior Olympic level and beyond, practice sessions will lengthen and increase in frequency. Adding pitches to her repertoire will also increase the length of practice sessions. But the pitcher need not throw every type of pitch in every practice. For older pitchers, practice five days a week is sufficient, with some days being heavier workouts than other days. Remember, the body and mind need time to rest and recover. If the pitcher works hard during practices, her body and mind will continue to progress even during rest periods.

I am not a big fan of counting pitches, but an average workout for a younger pitcher could be anywhere from 50 to 100 pitches, and for the older pitcher anywhere from 100 to 200 pitches, depending on the design of the practice. The pitcher should remember to work at maximum speed and effort when possible, that is, when she is not breaking something down and working on technique. Working at 75 percent effort will create muscle memory of 75 percent effort, which will soon become her maximum speed if she is not careful. When possible, workouts should end at full speed with 10 or 15 fastballs.

THREE TRAINING SEASONS

Every sport has three seasons—off-season, preseason, and in-season. No matter what an athlete is training to do, the current training season dictates the specific practice regimen. Each season has precise goals and contributes in a particular way to preparation and improvement (see figure 12.1).

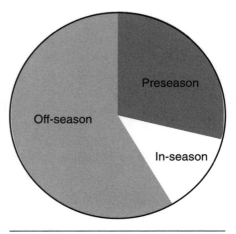

Figure 12.1 The growth possibilities of the three seasons.

Off-Season (September to December)

If you look at the graph, you will notice that the off-season covers the greatest area. This is appropriate because the off-season offers the pitcher the greatest opportunity for improvement and growth. I have to laugh to myself when a pitcher talks about taking the winter off and getting back into pitching in the spring. Off-season is the time to add a new pitch, work on speed within the motion, and break down the mechanics to repair problems. Off-season progress will determine what kind of pitcher will appear in-season.

Off-season is the time to go back to basics, whether that be with an old form or a new pitch. In the off-season the pitcher can isolate her skill work by repeating one type of pitch because she does not have to mix in other pitches in live situations. Moreover, because the season is still far away, the pitcher does not need to emphasize controlling and pinpointing the increased speed or new pitch.

Preseason (January to Mid-February)

If preparing to pitch were like baking a cake, off-season would be measuring, stirring, and mixing the ingredients. Preseason would be putting the cake in the oven. Preseason is the polishing of rough edges left over from the off-season. For instance, if the pitcher emphasized speed work in the off-season, preseason would be the time to add accuracy to the speed. If the pitcher learned to throw a change-up in the off-season, pre-season would be the time to start getting the pitch in the strike zone against hitters.

Preseason is preparing to play. Although the off-season affords the luxury of not having pressurized competition right around the corner, preseason does not. In fact, the imminent arrival of the season defines the theme of preseason training. Charting pitches for accuracy, weeding out pitches that were not mastered, mixing pitches, and creating realistic situations are all part of preseason training. This will be the final touch before the performance.

In-Season (Competition)

Going back to the cake analogy, in-season is eating the cake. All that the pitcher put into it, and the care she took (or did not take) to bake it just right, will come out now. It is really too late to go back and change the taste—it's baked.

Although in-season is the time when the pitcher works with what she has built over the last year, this period is still important to her growth as a pitcher. In-season will give her that vital, irreplaceable quality known as experience. No simulation of pressure or situation can match the real deal of live competitive action. During the season a pitcher learns

- to judge and read hitters,
- to feel a pitch work,
- to set up hitters,
- to work out of a jam (and to avoid that jam next time),
- to use the advantage of staying ahead in the count,
- to work through adverse situations such as tight strike zones and errors, and
- to put mental training such as focus points or pitch triggers to the test.

During the season the pitcher learns what she will need to work on in the off-season. Most of all, in-season is when a pitcher gains confidence in herself and her pitches. It is the time to reap the rewards of a disciplined year of training and to evaluate where to go next.

Training does not stop during the season; it just changes. Instead of building and inventing, the pitcher should polish her skills. She can identify areas she needs to work on based on game results. For instance, if the drop ball is cutting but simply starting too low, she should work on a higher release point in practice. Practice loads should be based on when the pitcher threw last in a game situation and when she will throw again.

Statistics such as the following are useful:

- Total pitches thrown each inning and total pitches thrown in the game
- Strikeouts, walks, and hits per game
- Types of pitches thrown for strikes, strikeouts, and balls
- Types of pitches thrown in the various count situations and the types of pitches thrown to get ahead or behind in the count

PITCHERS AND BATTING PRACTICE

How could I leave this one out? *Coaches must never use competitive pitchers to throw batting practice—ever!* Putting a pitcher out on the mound and telling her to "just throw it in there and let them hit it so the batters can get confidence off a live arm" is like putting hitters in the box and instructing them to "just swing and miss really hard so the pitcher can get confidence off a live hitter." How much sense does that make?

The coach who wants a live arm should use his or her own arm. First, pitchers should never work on grooving the ball. Second, a pitcher's makeup, ego, self-confidence, and all that good stuff are shot when she is asked to be noncompetitive and allow someone to hit the ball. That scenario could compare to a boxer allowing himself to be punched in the face. Third, it is dangerous to put the pitcher on the mound and have her groove the ball down the middle. Ever hear of "in the middle, out the middle"? The more often a pitcher chucks one down Broadway, the more likely it is that a hard line drive will come blazing up the middle.

If the coach wants the team to have batting practice and "gain confidence," then he or she should have a staff member pitch from behind a screen or use a pitching machine (that's what they are for). If the coach wants pitchers to work against hitters and hitters to see realistic pitches, then the catcher should go behind the plate and the battery should work as if they are in a game situation, calling pitches and trying for strikeouts. That sort of practice will be beneficial to everyone.

FORMULATING A GAME PLAN

Going into any game, the pitcher, catcher, and coach should have formulated a plan of attack by considering the pitcher's strengths and the nature and strengths of the opposing hitters. Developing a strategy will put a thought process in place that will implement rationale and reason into the pitch calling.

The first element to look at is what kind of team the pitcher is facing. The following are some of the questions to consider:

- Does this team bunt or not? If so, do they bunt by the book (runner on first base with no outs or one out)? If the game is close, do they squeeze bunt?
- Will this team steal often? If so, who, when, and which bases?
- What is this team's particular offensive style? Big hitters? Slap and run? Or a combination of both?
- If the game is at their park, what type of environment and atmosphere will be present?

The next thing to look at are the tendencies of individual hitters. The following are some of the questions to ask:

- Do they have a good eye for balls and strikes? Will they take a first pitch? Will they take good pitches or swing at bad ones?
- Do they strike out swinging or taking? Which pitches will they fish for? Do they protect the plate well with two strikes?
- Do they have the discipline to wait for their pitch, or will they swing at any strike in the zone?
- Does the slapper run toward the pitcher or away toward first base? Can the slapper also swing away and hit for power?

- Are they good bunters? Can they bunt for a base hit? Will they pop up the rise ball when attempting to bunt?
- Are they good in clutch situations, or do they choke when the pressure is on?
- Do they have mechanical weaknesses such as high hands, low hands, faulty location or position of stance, incorrect stride length or location, sweeping swings, upper cuts, or chop swings?

Finally, in making a game plan, the pitcher should set personal goals, which should be realistic and have a next option if the original goal becomes unattainable. For instance, if the goal is a perfect game and the pitcher walks a batter in the first inning, she resets her goal to throw a no-hitter. The following are some examples of personal goal setting.

- No hits, no walks, or no runs
- Get ahead and stay ahead of the hitters
- Get the first batter of each inning out
- No errors
- No one gets past second or third
- No multiple hits or extra-base hits

Any one or combination of these will work. The important thing is to remember the mission.

One last point to remember is that the kind of pitch thrown can affect the result or location of the hit. For instance, if the pitcher wants a ground ball, she should keep the pitch down or throw drop balls. If she wants the left side of the field to make a defensive play (perhaps the strong arm in left field can prevent the runner from scoring on a sacrifice fly, or the shortstop is a vacuum cleaner on ground balls, or the third baseman is outstanding at fielding the bunt), then she should keep the ball on the inside half of the plate to a right-handed hitter. If the pitcher wants the right side of the field to make a defensive play, then she should keep the ball on the outside of the plate to a right-handed hitter. Some of these possibilities never cross the minds of the battery and coach, but these sorts of situations could quite possibly affect the outcome of the game.

PREGAME WARM-UP

Most pitchers, it seems, either overdo the warm-up or fail to perform an adequate one. I believe this occurs because many pitchers have no idea of their goals for warming up. A warm-up is the pitcher's preparation to compete—a preparation of the pitches she will use during the game to ensure their effectiveness.

Many pitchers mistakenly think that the purpose of the warm-up is simply to warm up their muscles so that they can pitch hard without being injured. That is only a small fraction of the goal. The big picture also includes these objectives:

- The pitcher wants to be sure that she is fundamentally sound. Sometimes a fundamental technique can inadvertently become distorted. Any number of circumstances may be the cause. For instance, the ground on the last field may have been uneven or rough where the stride foot was supposed to land, so the pitcher changed her power line and compromised a little control and efficiency to avoid stepping into a hole on every pitch. That adjustment may have stuck. Or perhaps the pitcher has been throwing a lot of innings and fatigue has caused her back leg to become lazy so that it is not driving into the pitch well. That modification may have stuck. The time to check for proper technique and to eliminate the odd mistake is during the pregame warm-up.

- The pitcher should be sure that all pitches are ready and working, or at least identify the pitches she is struggling with. She should start pitches close and slow in warm-ups to get everything right. Then she can add distance and speed. A pitcher may be excited and impatient and just start throwing all the junk at full speed, never making sure that things are right first. She must be patient and have goals in warming up. If the pitcher performs the warm-up properly, chances are that she will eliminate many of the problems that can occur from game to game with a certain pitch.

The way a pitcher prepares will more than likely signal the way she performs. If every change-up in warm-ups is way out of the zone, it is unlikely that in the game they will all suddenly become strikes.

Finally, every pitcher should take responsibility to be prepared to pitch. The coach should tell the pitchers before the warm-up who is the starter, the first reliever, and if possible the second reliever. Coaches should not keep this information secret. From there, *it is the responsibility of the pitcher to be warmed up and prepared to go in at any time.*

The need to relieve a pitcher is usually unforeseeable. A coach is not psychic so is unlikely to say, "Erica is starting and she will pitch pretty well until the fifth inning when, without warning, she will blow up, so be ready." The responsibility of the coach is to tell a pitcher whether she is in relief or not and to get the players to the park with ample time to warm up. The responsibility of the pitcher is to be ready to go into the game at any time and pitch effectively.

Pitching is a position that cannot be performed haphazardly. The pitcher should be alert and always aware of what is going on in the game, with her own team as well as the opposing hitters. An aloof pitcher will be unprepared to pitch her own game, much less to relieve someone else. Pitchers should strive for a businesslike approach to their role in the outcome of the game. Much rides on their performance. It is a shame when lack of preparation causes failure.

The moral of the story is to be prepared. The better a pitcher prepares for competition, the better she will compete, and the more she will win. Good routines contribute to good preparation in both practice and pregame. With the help and advice of coaches, the pitcher has the responsibility to form and implement good practice routines and game preparation. But she and her coaches must also keep workouts varied and challenging. No one enjoys the same old thing time after time. The pitcher should set goals for her drills and practices and remember to emphasize quality instead of quantity.

MENTAL MAKEUP

13

Many aspects contribute to the mental makeup of the pitcher. Some of the components are solid routines that the pitcher can practice and master. Some of the aspects are less tangible but contribute just as powerfully to the pitcher's approach to the game. The outcome of a game results largely from the effectiveness of the pitcher. Much has been said about the quirkiness, cockiness, and uniqueness of pitchers. Many coaches take a surface impression and unfortunately never go beyond that. Coaches should take a closer look at what goes into making a pitcher mentally strong and able to accept the steep responsibilities that go with the position.

MENTAL PRACTICE

One of the most effective ways of practicing involves the mental component. In the middle of practicing, a pitcher may find it almost impossible to perform a movement or make an adjustment. This occurs because the body is probably reverting to muscle memory and performing a movement different from what is desired. When this happens, physically trying to repeat an adjustment is sometimes pointless.

This is a good time for the pitcher to walk away and think through the adjustment and movements necessary for the desired move or correction. She should take some time—a couple of minutes or a couple of days—to think about what is currently happening and what movements she would like to perform. The progress that players can make by thinking through the adjustment can be surprising.

This method is a shadow of the big picture of the mental training necessary for any successful athlete. Imagery, visualization, and positive thinking will go a long way toward developing self-confidence and belief in oneself. Players can use down time during the day or before falling asleep to get in some mental practice.

MOUND PRESENCE

An important part of being a good pitcher is having presence on the mound. A pitcher's confidence, concentration, and command of the position will project an air of intimidation to opposing hitters. The way a pitcher handles herself will hint at whether she can be hit, shaken, or beaten. If the opposing team believes they cannot hit, they will not hit. If they believe a pitcher cannot be rattled, they will not try to rattle her. And if they believe they cannot beat a pitcher, they will not beat her. If by appearance and action a pitcher can manipulate her opponent, she has a formidable advantage.

Pitchers such as Lisa Fernandez emanate confidence and composure from the mound.

Pitchers learn early—some of them the hard way—that they must focus on the task at hand and block out everything else. The better a pitcher is and the more success she has, the more she will be hounded and heckled by the opposing crowd and team—until they realize that it's not working. The pitcher must learn to *throw one pitch at a time* and concentrate on the most important thing right now, which is the next pitch.

In instructing a pitcher through drills and exercises, I try to help the pitcher condition her mind to think about one thing at a time. Whether the task is stepping on a power line, holding the head up straight, or following through loosely, the goal for the pitcher is to focus her mind on that particular objective. Pitchers who have this ability exhibit a much more important positive quality than they immediately realize. These pitchers will be able to lock their minds into pitching when the heat of competition is upon them. The trait that permits a pitcher to make physical adjustments in practice will contribute to mental toughness in competition!

TRIGGERS AND ROUTINES

In chapter 12 we discussed routines in practice and pregame. Routines are also extremely helpful during the game. Linking the game routine to the practice routine can help the pitcher relax and feel comfortable with what is going on. If a pitcher reacts in a much different way during a game than she does in practice, then she has no level of comfort or familiarity when the pressure is at its height.

Remember the importance of having a focus point to lock on to—the small target the size of a bug? That device is a simple example of a routine—focusing on a small target area and "locking in." Triggers are also helpful. A trigger is a cue such as a visual or oral reminder that helps the pitcher execute the correct action. For instance, a pitcher who is throwing her change-up too high may imagine dropping the change-up on home plate to make it come down lower in the strike zone. That image would be her trigger. A pitcher usually figures out her triggers in practice or pregame warm-up and briefly repeats them to herself after seeing the signal to throw that particular pitch.

Simulation of Pressure

Another routine that I encourage is the simulation of pressure. At the end of basketball practice, our coach used to have all players line up on the baseline. Every player would shoot one free throw. If the player missed, we ran a suicide. If the player made it, we did nothing. I have heard critics say that this sort of negative reinforcement does not work positively toward a common goal. I believe it sets a routine that effectively simulates pressure situations when otherwise there is no pressure, such as in practice.

Simulating the pressure of competition and performance is difficult to accomplish in a positive way. To most competitors, losing is a negative. But the coach should not allow the experience of losing to be the only time an athlete undergoes pressure and has to manage it. Therefore, creating pressure situations in practice is necessary. Some pitchers can do this in their own mind by re-creating the feelings and anxiety they experience when the game is on the line. Others, however, need the help of coaches to create external pressure with some type of negative consequence. If this pressure becomes familiar, the pitcher will react positively when necessary.

Let me offer another lesson from my days of playing basketball as a youngster. My brother and I spent countless hours in the backyard shooting baskets in our make-believe games. Without fail, when one of us picked up the ball the other one would start counting down, "Three . . . two . . . one," to imitate the clock ticking down and time running out. The person with the ball would be forced to shoot a hurried, pressured, last-second shot. We did this hundreds of times. In my career as a basketball player, I took that last-second shot twice when the game was on the line. Some people find it difficult to imagine that at those moments I *wanted* the ball. You see, I *knew* I could make it. I had made it a hundred times in my backyard! Other players on that court did not want the ball because—you guessed it—they had never made that shot or even tried it.

Game Routine

We talked before about practice routines. Now let's take a look at the following example of an on-field game routine that can sharpen the pitcher's mental approach. With a little practice, the pitcher can implement this routine and gain some consistency, comfort, and positive reaction to pressure situations. The locations simply show the order in which the pitcher thinks; she does not need to duplicate them exactly. Imagine a pitcher on the rubber pitching, finishing out front, and returning to the back of the rubber to make the approach for the next pitch (see figure 13.1).

1. Taking the signal. To prepare to pitch, the first thing the pitcher does is take the signal from the catcher. This act initiates the rest of the process.

2. Location and trigger. By considering the count, the pitcher will know whether to throw the pitch in the red, yellow, or green zone. She should use a trigger to help in execution. Some pitchers take a deep breath here. They may think about triggering when they inhale and committing to the pitch as they exhale.

3. Throwing the pitch.

4. Analysis and count. After throwing the pitch, the pitcher will have an automatic reaction of good or bad. The pitcher should then note whether she is ahead or behind in the count.

5. Feeling and correction. If the pitch worked, the pitcher should have a good feeling about it. If the pitch did not work (such as a drop ball hanging), the pitcher should think of what went wrong and what the

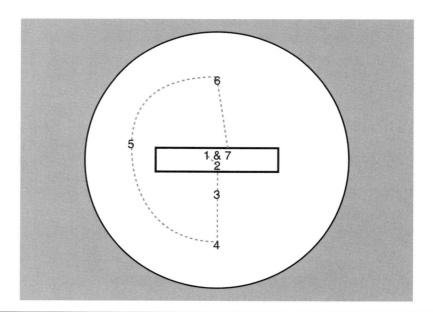

Figure 13.1 The mental circle of the pitch.

correction is (such as getting over the front foot sooner). This will set up the trigger for the next time the catcher calls that particular pitch.

6. Clearing the pitch. I have this one located off the back of the rubber because the pitcher should not even think about approaching the next pitch without clearing the last one—good or bad. Clearing the pitch simply means that the pitcher gets it off her mind so that she can devote total attention to the pitch she is about to throw. Some pitchers like to draw a line in the dirt behind the rubber to signify the boundary that they will not cross until they have cleared the pitch.

7. Taking the signal. The whole process starts again.

This may seem like a complicated procedure, but once a pitcher gets the structure, it becomes automatic. The process can occur on a smooth walk back to the rubber and should not appear to take any extra time. If a pitcher has an effective mental circle, she will always be focused.

MENTALLY PREPARING TO PITCH

The goal for mental preparation is the same as physical preparation: to be as ready as possible to compete successfully. Through mental preparation, a pitcher can relieve anxiety, familiarize herself with the opponent's lineup, and begin to focus on the game.

One of the overlooked methods of preparation, especially among younger pitchers (those not at the college level), is scouting and becoming familiar with the opposing team's lineup. The pitcher may be playing another position or sitting on the bench and because she is not pitching, pays no attention to how certain hitters are reacting to pitches. Pitchers should remember that they could be facing the same hitters in the future—a future that may be an inning away, a few games away, or a month away. Whatever the circumstance, information on hitters' tendencies can contribute mightily to the pitcher's success in handling them.

Whether the pitcher is the starter or a possible reliever will determine her level of adrenaline, but there is not a big difference in mental preparation. Although the relief pitcher does not have the pressure of the current situation, she can count on experiencing pressure when she enters the game. The relief pitcher has the advantage of being able to observe the hitters in action before she faces them herself. The information she collects will be helpful in deciding what approach to take with each hitter.

Pitchers should be aware of the players in the opponent's lineup. Of course, it would be nice to know the likes and dislikes of individual hitters, but such information is not always available. The pitcher should realize that the structure of the lineup tends to put certain types of hitters in certain places. We can make the following generalizations about a lineup:

1. Leadoff hitter—Tendency to be fast, bunt well, and have a high on-base percentage.

2. Second hitter—Good bunter. Usually has some speed and bunts often in sacrifice situations.

3. Third hitter—The third, fourth, and fifth hitters usually have the highest batting averages on the team. The third hitter may have some versatility with speed and bunting capability as well as a high batting average and ability to drive in runners.

4. Cleanup hitter—Usually a powerful hitter, not a bunter. May be an all-or-nothing hitter who would have a high probability of either hitting a home run or striking out.

5. Five hitter—Good solid hitter. Many pitchers start to relax after number four. The five hitter's ability will dictate whether the pitcher must throw to number four or not. This hitter usually has less speed and more power.

6.–9. The hitting ability of players in the lower part of the lineup can vary. Many teams do not have a lot of depth offensively, so after the fourth or fifth hitter, the pitcher begins to face weaker hitters with lower batting averages. Against stronger teams and deeper lineups, however, the six and seven hitters will have power potential but probably lower batting averages than the hitters in the top half of the lineup. The eight and nine hitters will tend to have speed and bunting and slapping ability that may get them on base for the top of the lineup.

Obviously, this is not a foolproof system, but it will give the pitcher an idea of what to expect. If a hitter does not have characteristics typical of her spot in the lineup, that is something to remember. Pitchers often pitch the same way to every hitter with no apparent rationale and no anticipation of what may be happening at the plate or on the bases.

EFFECTS OF OFFENSE AND DEFENSE

One successful college coach tells his pitchers to "keep the opposition under five runs and we'll win." What an incredible feeling that must be for the pitcher! Knowing that the offense is committed to scoring runs gives the pitcher room to breathe. A mistake does not always cost her the game. Although that particular pitching staff rarely gives up five runs or anything close to it, the point is that from the outset the coach greatly reduces the pressure on the pitcher. A pitcher can relax and trust herself, pitching to her potential, rather than have to pitch carefully and cautiously in trying to avoid mistakes.

Right or wrong, a competitive pitcher's approach is different when the team does not function effectively behind her. I once had a coach tell me that his pitchers (who were excellent drop-ball pitchers) were suddenly throwing an abundance of pitches in the dirt, even before the plate. He wondered what had suddenly gone wrong. I pointed out to him that his team was averaging seven errors a game. The pitchers no doubt felt as if they had the burden of striking out every batter. Consequently, they were forcing their pitches to move or break to keep them out of the hitters' zones. Wild pitches in the direction of the intended movement, in this case downward, were the result.

That scenario is a pretty standard one. Pitchers who have a defense behind them that makes errors, an offense that does not score runs, or a catcher who cannot throw out runners at second base feel pressured to not allow a single runner to reach first. Although keeping runners off base may be a common goal at the outset of the game or inning, the pitcher does not want to feel that she is always facing a do-or-die situation.

Pitchers who find themselves in that circumstance must understand where their job ends. If the pitcher strikes out a hitter and the catcher drops the third strike to allow the runner to reach first, the pitcher must recover and realize that she did her job. She must deal with the new situation and acknowledge that the mistake was not hers. Likewise, if a teammate misplays a routine ground ball or pop fly, the pitcher should know that she has executed her job well. The teamwork involved in softball plays a big role in the outcome of the game. The pitcher directly affects only the pitches she throws and the plays she makes.

The ability to shut out distractions and focus on the task at hand is an important one for pitchers.

The ability to recover from mistakes and refocus on the current task is essential. The pitcher must first analyze what is within her control. Other players, the lineup, the weather, the umpire, the coach, parents, and so on are *not* within the pitcher's control. We have spent a lot of time on routines, triggers, and focus points of pitching. Those are the things that the pitcher controls. Pitchers should use those tools and approach adverse situations with control and composure.

On the other hand, a team that scores runs, makes plays, and works well together allows their pitcher to throw her game without the pressure of always being in a tight situation or feeling that she is a failure if she allows a base runner. A confident pitcher can throw the pitch without having to think "What if it goes in the outfield?" or "What if she bunts it to our third baseman?" The confident pitcher realizes that if the ball goes into play, her fielders will do their job and the outcome will probably be favorable.

FINDING WHAT WORKS

The pitcher should use mental methods that are comfortable to her and not forced. I was the type of pitcher who woke up, literally, when the van pulled into the parking lot at the game. I was relaxed and loose before the game, almost carefree. During the game, I looked around between pitches—at my teammates, the on-deck batter, the action in the bullpen, and so on. I might even watch a plane flying over. But I was not unfocused. I knew the situation of the game. When the pitch was called, I always saw the pitch work in my mind before I started the windup. But my appearance was loose and relaxed.

In 1995, after having been retired for a year, I decided to come back for the final Olympic softball trial. To do that, I put myself under the most rigorous physical and mental programs I could find. I had never used mental training before. Everything had come naturally for me. Now I was listening to motivational tapes when I woke up, before I went to bed, and a couple of times in between. I had motivational songs on a cassette tape that I listened to in my dorm room (at the tryout), on the bus on the way to the field, and during any down time we had between activities. Although this was all well-intentioned coaching, it did not work for me. By the time I got the ball in my hand, I was pumped up, motivated, and a nervous wreck! I had gone totally away from the routines that had worked for me for 20 years.

This story is not meant to steer anyone away from mental training. I tell it only to urge coaches and players to realize that not every athlete is the same. Different athletes need different types of mental training. The key is to find something that works and stick to it.

Finally, because mental aspects are not obviously visible, pitchers and coaches often underestimate and overlook them. As you have seen in this chapter, there is a lot going on in a pitcher's mind that contributes to everything from the practice field to game situations in either a positive or a negative way. Recognizing the importance of a strong mental approach is half the battle. A pitcher who understands the role of mental training will continue to build a strong foundation that will contribute to her overall performance.

PHYSICAL CONDITIONING 14

Physical conditioning is another piece of the pie that can contribute greatly to the pitcher's success. A completely trained pitcher will have completed not only technical training in fundamentals and mechanics but also mental and physical training. Although the three seasons of training (off-season, preseason, and in-season) shape the workout schedule, the pitcher will find in each of the three phases an area in which to progress. The three primary ways to strength train in relation to pitching are practical training (sport specific and position specific), traditional training (weights, plyometrics, aerobics, etc.), and cross-sport training (participating in sports other than softball).

PRACTICAL TRAINING

Practical training involves exercises or drills that place the pitcher in the pitching motion or any part of it while strengthening all or part of the motion itself. The pitcher should use this type of training whenever possible because it not only builds strength but incorporates that strength specifically into the pitching motion.

Practical training examples and drills appear throughout this book, many in the mechanics and fundamentals sections. Working on fundamentals often calls for the isolation of a certain movement. Such drills add strength to a specific area while also training the muscles to repeat the movements. The following drills have those characteristics:

- Double and triple arm circles work on strengthening the arm and speeding up the circle through repetition (page 68).
- Speed drills for time improve both endurance and fast-twitch muscle response (pages 69–70).
- Distance pitching strengthens the pitcher by requiring greater effort than young pitchers typically use to throw 35 or 40 feet.
- Weighted-ball workouts develop power and strength and then add speed to the newly developed power by using underweighted and over-weighted balls (pages 70–71).

- Harness training, whether with a full-body harness or just an ankle harness on the drive leg, strengthens and conditions the body to move faster by assisting or resisting movement (pages 70–73).
- Tossing a football over distance reinforces the whipping of the arm and strengthens the arm within the whip (pages 42–43).

These are just a few of the drills that incorporate strength training in a practical way. Here are a couple others that will isolate the drive leg and consequently increase power.

PRACTICE IT ## One-to-One Drill

In this drill the pitcher stands balanced on the drive leg. Bending slightly as if preparing to jump, she powers outward with the stride, beginning with the thigh or quad of the drive leg rather than the foot or leg of the stride leg. Some pitchers will feel awkward when first trying this drill because they are not accustomed to using their legs to incorporate power. They start the motion simply by stepping forward comfortably. By starting the drill with the drive leg, the body will start to count on the contribution of power, thus generating more speed overall. Once the pitcher has pitched the ball, she should balance on her stride leg. The pitch goes from one leg (the drive leg) to the other leg (the stride leg). Isolation for strengthening is a factor, and balance is incorporated.

PRACTICE IT ## Brace Drill

Like the one-to-one drill, the brace drill isolates the drive leg to enhance power and strength. The pitcher positions the drive leg against something solid. In

Jennie Finch shows that the movements involved in pitching require proper conditioning of the body to optimize performance and avoid injury.

pitching lessons and clinics we sometimes use a base, but many objects will work, including a stair. The pitcher braces the drive leg against the object and shifts most of her weight over the drive leg. This will leave the stride leg barely touching the ground. (If she is bracing against a stair, she lightly touches the next stair with her stride leg.) She again begins the stride, using the thigh or quad of the drive leg (against the brace) to power outward. She finishes the pitch normally. In both of these drills, the emphasis is not on the length of the stride but on the force in getting to the stride leg powerfully.

In practical strength training, correct mechanics are obviously important. Adding strength by using incorrect movements only strengthens the mistake.

TRADITIONAL TRAINING

Traditional strength training includes the obvious approaches that most people associate with getting stronger or working out. Weight training, plyometrics, aerobics, body-weight exercises, and so on are included in this category, with weight training being the most common. *To lift weights correctly, the athlete must use a great deal of technique.* Unless the athlete learns and practices the techniques, weight-training exercises can be harmful rather than helpful.

Weight training should be customized to the individual. The pitcher should have the help of a professional to advise on technique and consult for workout length, types of exercises, and so on. The following are some helpful tips for pitchers involved in weight training.

- The appropriate weight is 75 to 80 percent of the maximum weight load for the athlete on that particular exercise.
- The pitcher should perform greater numbers of reps, such as two sets of 12 or thee sets of 10, rather than fewer reps or a downward progression of reps, such as 10, 8, and 6 over three sets.
- The pitcher should remind trainers who may be offering professional advice that flexibility is important to her effectiveness.
- Stretching or flexing is appropriate before working out to warm up the muscles and at the end of a workout to help maintain flexibility. The athlete must be sure to avoid overstretching, which can lessen elasticity. Elasticity within the muscles, specifically the muscles in the arm, contributes to whipping potential. In addition, joint integrity is determined by some degree of elasticity within the muscles and connective tissue.
- When performing the bench press, athletes should go no farther than 90 degrees with the arm angle. Athletes often learn a bench-press technique that allows the bar to touch the chest. That position forces the elbows past the shoulder plane and increases the risk that impingement will occur.

In traditional strength training, body-weight exercises are an excellent way to strengthen. Body-weight exercises like push-ups, crunches, dips, pull-ups, and so on are simple exercises that are easy to perform and do not require the equipment and atmosphere needed for weight lifting. The pitcher can do body-weight exercises in her home, at the field, and elsewhere. She must be careful to avoid impingement on the push-ups by not going beyond 90 degrees with the arms. The back must not drop below the shoulders. The old routine of touching the nose to the ground is definitely out for pitchers.

Resistance tube training is another method that does not require a certain setting or a lot of equipment. Many good exercises that use the bands and tubing are available to strengthen and isolate connective tissue and smaller muscle groups. These smaller muscle groups and connective tissue are often where the initial breakdown occurs for injuries.

CROSS-SPORT TRAINING

Whether competing on a recreational or competitive level, the pitcher can benefit from participating in sports other than softball. Other sports require her to use muscles in a different way. Competing in other sports develops such factors as reaction quickness, fast-twitch muscle firing, foot speed, endurance, and body awareness in making certain movements. Multisport athletes develop coordination at a young age in many different areas rather than in a single constant motion or movement.

We discussed previously the need for pitchers to be dedicated and committed to their position. To accomplish this, they may have to limit their involvement in other sports, but this limitation does not include recreational sports and activities. The pitcher should not underestimate the advantages of jogging, swimming, skiing, cycling, skating, and the many team sports that can be played in pickup games, in the backyard, or at the gym. Ping-pong is an excellent recreational sport that develops reactions and quickness: two qualities necessary in defending the position closest to the hitter.

CONDITIONING GUIDELINES

Here are some other things to keep in mind that pertain to the physical conditioning of the pitcher.

Overweight athletes and poor nutrition.   Because of the makeup of the body, an overweight pitcher must make different movements in the delivery of the underhand pitch. These modified movements allow her to make the delivery but are often fundamentally incorrect. Pitchers, like all athletes, should attempt to eat right and supply their bodies with the nutrition they need to perform the demands of their sport. The overweight pitcher should not be afraid to consult a professional to deal with weight problems and nutrition.

Researching pitching philosophies and sticking to one.   Many pitchers work under the philosophy of more is better. They expose themselves to everything available in the area of learning to pitch. Improvement and change are, of course, part of the process of development, but the pitcher must have some consistency in her training. Pitchers have come to me on a Tuesday for a lesson, during which I tell them they need to drive the back leg more, and then on Friday they see another coach who tells them that the back leg is not important. This situation does not help the pitcher. She must have consistency in workout goals that do not change according to the day of the week! The pitcher should find a reputable pitching instructor or clinician and stay committed.

Contribution of rest and down time to the development of strength. Athletes must allow their bodies opportunities to recuperate and become stronger. Rest or down time gives the body an opportunity to heal and develop new and stronger muscles. Rest also gives the mind a chance to recover from the strain of concentration. Certain days (usually two) of the week should be considered off days. The pitcher also benefits by allowing her body to rest for several weeks after the traditional season of competition. She must not be afraid to rest. Sometimes rest does more good than anything.

The pitcher should be creative with her strength workouts. If she enjoys time away from pitching, traditional or cross-sport training will fit into her schedule just fine. If she does not particularly enjoy that type of training or is restricted by time allotments for workouts, practical training will probably fit better into her plan. As you can see, the approach to physical conditioning of the pitcher can take many forms. The player should feel free to mix and match and remember the importance of being well rounded in her development as a pitcher.

15 COMMUNICATION

Communication is an underlying element of our everyday lives. The pitcher should think of trying to go through a normal school day without the communication of class times, locations, homework assignments, test directions, who to sit by at lunch, and so on. Without communication, chaos would dominate. No one could work together because organization would be absent.

Softball also relies heavily on communication to avoid chaos. The number of outs, the count, the inning, player positions, the batting order, and so on keep the game going smoothly and the teams working toward a common goal. Teams who take it a step further and run plays on defense, set up an offense to score, and work pitch counts to batters will see even more success through their efforts.

Pitching is no exception in the reliance on communication. Pitchers need to know pitch-calling strategy, the count, the hitter's history, and the strike zone, just to mention a few points. The better the pitcher can communicate, the more information she will have on which to base her plan of action. The pitcher uses three essential sets of communication lines in her on-field relationships during the game. These lines of communication run between

- pitcher and catcher,
- pitcher and coach, and
- pitcher and umpire.

PITCHER AND CATCHER

In chapter 11 we discussed in depth the importance of a good catcher. I will add here that the relationship between the members of the battery should be the tightest relationship on the field. As mentioned earlier, off the field those two players do not have to be best friends or bosom buddies. They do not even have to like each other. But on the field they should have respect for each other's jobs and a common goal to succeed.

The catcher and pitcher can communicate in many ways. They can talk face to face in the dugout between innings, a form of communication that should be common practice. After each inning, the pitcher and catcher can step aside in the dugout and discuss the inning that just passed, the effectiveness or lack of effectiveness of pitches, upcoming hitters, and so forth. This discussion should not be strained or forced but just be a normal conversation that deals specifically with the current task.

The pitcher and catcher can communicate nonverbally on the field. A pitcher can shake off a pitch, nod or signal for a certain pitch call, or acknowledge the catcher on a good call, catch, or throw. The catcher, in turn, can signal a certain pitch, suggest a slight adjustment on a pitch, or gesture positively after a good pitch or strikeout. All of this communication can occur with little or no oral communication between the two.

Pitchers often fail to acknowledge the catcher after a strikeout. Many top pitchers gesture to the catcher on strike three. This gesture or acknowledgment is because they realize that the calls were good, that the catcher did her job in completing the strikeout by catching and framing the ball or hanging on to a pitch that was not exactly routine.

Along those lines, remember that a foul tip that is missed is a foul ball. A foul tip that is caught is a strike. If the catcher does not do her job and hang

One of the lines of communication runs between the pitcher and the catcher. They must trust each other and share common goals.

on to the foul tip, the pitcher does not get the strikeout. So the pitcher's acknowledgement of a caught foul tip is particularly appropriate.

Finally, the pitcher and catcher can talk on the mound during the inning. This conference is an opportunity to eliminate confusion about a situation or settle down and regroup. The catcher can give the pitcher some confidence or simply tell her to find her head! The pitcher and catcher should keep these discussions to a minimum because they can disrupt the rhythm and focus of both the pitcher and the entire defense.

Some pitchers respond well to aggression. Others need almost constant reassurance. No one can better read this and know how to respond in a certain situation than the person directly in front of the pitcher. Effective communication between the catcher and the pitcher will eliminate many problems and make it easier to attain common objectives.

PITCHER AND COACH

The most common phrase heard by coaches about pitchers is this: "Pitchers— you can't live with 'em, and you can't live without 'em." Pitchers are often known for their cockiness, arrogance, and selfishness. In their defense, they spend countless hours working on perfection and tolerating demanding coaches and parents. If they are good, they are a target for heckles, insults, and harassment from the moment they step into the circle, no matter what their age. The better they are, the rougher it gets.

None of that is an excuse; it is simply a brief explanation of how some mind-sets and attitudes arise. Show me a thin-skinned pitcher, and I will show you a pitcher who can be rattled right off the mound. The coach must realize why pitchers are made the way they are, where they have come from to be where they are, and what it will take for them to withstand the battles ahead.

The most important issue between the coach and the pitcher is communication. I have heard countless stories of pitchers who are afraid to tell a coach that their arm is sore, that they would like to throw more than two change-ups a game, that they need more time to warm up, that their finger is too sore to throw the rise ball effectively on a particular day, or any number of other concerns that could considerably affect the outcome of the game. Because the coach is the adult (usually), the responsibility falls on him or her to be certain that the pitcher is comfortable enough to communicate problems or concerns at any time.

The coach should become familiar with the physical strengths and weaknesses of the pitcher, especially if the coach is calling the pitches. In regard to pitch calling, the coach should know the execution percentage of each target and each movement pitch, discuss scouting reports before the game, discuss strengths and weaknesses of the pitcher on that particular day, and allow the pitcher to shake off a pitch if she feels strongly about it.

A coach should know a pitcher's comfort zone, if she is better as a starter or a reliever or if it matters, and how she responds to pressure situations. Like the catcher, the coach who notices a problem or anticipates a reaction from the pitcher may be able to prevent a negative situation or enhance a positive one.

Coaches should include pitchers in team practice when possible. Some coaches isolate their pitchers and do not work them into practice situations to learn plays such as cutoffs, backups, and typical ground-ball plays with runners on base. This oversight can lead to big mistakes in games, for which the pitcher may ultimately feel responsible. Isolating the pitchers also separates them emotionally from the rest of the team.

Finally, the coach and pitcher must share an understanding of what it will take to succeed with a certain hitter, in a certain game, or at a certain level. For instance, a pitcher may be getting 14 strikeouts per game but giving up a home run or two in the process. The pitcher may look at the strikeout column and think to herself that she is doing fine and that her team needs to score more runs. The coach may need to communicate that although the strikeout count is terrific, the home runs and long balls are a problem. The team may be playing at a level where one or two runs is the margin between a win and a loss. If this conversation never occurs, you have a frustrated coach, a frustrated pitcher, and, more than likely, a situation that is not improving.

PITCHER AND UMPIRE

Obviously, in an overall view of the game you would like the pitcher and umpire to have a good relationship. Complaining to or challenging the umpire will not foster a positive relationship and is unlikely to help with a particular call. Much of the pitcher-umpire communication is unspoken, and the pitcher has the sole responsibility to establish it.

The first thing the pitcher must do is search for the perimeters of the strike zone. We all know what the rulebook defines as the strike zone. We also know that every umpire has his or her own strike zone. So in the early innings the pitcher will have to explore the edges and see exactly where the zone starts and stops. After the pitcher has a relatively good idea, she works from there. She establishes the location of the green, yellow, and red zones for the game and throws accordingly. The pitcher should not make herself miserable for seven innings by arguing for a knee-high strike that the umpire, in the first inning, indicated would be a ball.

If a pitcher is capable of hitting targets effectively, she should establish that right away. By throwing more clear strikes in the early innings, she proves to the umpire that she can throw the ball where she wants to and can hit the zone at will. This display may cause the umpire to trust her to be accurate and to lean in her favor on borderline pitches.

Imagine two scenarios. One pitcher starts the game very accurately, throwing many strikes and hitting targets. The other pitcher starts the game wild. She is throwing balls in the dirt, getting behind hitters, grossly missing targets, and so forth. In a crucial situation later in the game with the count full and the bases loaded, the borderline pitch may tend to be a called strike for the first pitcher and ball four for the second pitcher. The umpire will often go with the pitcher's tendencies.

PITCHER AND PARENT

Having mentioned the three relationships that deal directly with on-the-field situations, we address here one that can also have a tremendous bearing on the mental and physical performance of the pitcher.

In fastpitch softball, parents often play an integral role in the development of the pitcher. We previously discussed approaches to practice situations, but we should also mention a few other aspects.

During the game, parents should allow the coach to communicate with the pitcher about strategies. The rewards of a solid pitcher-catcher relationship that has been nurtured through off-season practicing should also come to the fore during competition. Parents should allow the pitcher to perform to the best of her abilities and resist trying to affect every move she makes. The pitcher will surely make some mistakes, but parents should understand that no one in her situation can be perfect. A pitcher will gain much more from a mistake if she has learned to evaluate herself without constant dialogue and guidance from a parent.

It is no crime for a parent to offer advice when it is asked for or needed. But parents should avoid micromanaging the pitcher. They must trust her to trust herself. Discussion can occur later about the positives and negatives of the pitches, the outcome, and things to improve on.

Pitchers should also keep lines of communication open with parents. In a solid, healthy relationship, a parent can help a pitcher grow. An overzealous parent, however, can make participation in the sport miserable for his or her daughter. Parents must know when to stop communicating and how to let go of the game situation. Pitchers should be responsive to suggestions and discussion, and parents should be careful about choosing when and how long to discuss the game.

Although a parent can play a vital role in the development of the pitcher by helping her practice, the pitcher must accept equal responsibility. The relationship is often too dependent from the start, with a parent doing all of the practice catching, calling pitches from the stands, and yelling out corrections during or after each pitch. These actions are not only aggravating and annoying at the time but also tend to create a pitcher who does not know how to react and respond to situations on her own. This does nothing to develop the long-term maturity of the athlete.

In a team sport with on-field coaches, forming a solid network of understanding will be the first step in creating a successful team. Pitchers should not be afraid to share their feelings with catchers, coaches, or parents. Done effectively, communication will relieve anxiety and build confidence.

THE FINAL PITCH

Fastpitch softball is an exciting, action-packed, and challenging sport to play, coach, and watch. Over the last quarter century, the game has evolved into a popular college and Olympic sport. People who watch even one game often become fans for life. Television is recognizing the popularity of the sport worldwide, and opportunities for young female athletes in the sport are overwhelming.

I consider myself one of the lucky ones. I make a living in the sport I have loved since I first played it at age nine. I am grateful to the athletes who have trusted me with their development. I am proud of the coaches who dedicate themselves to getting it right and helping athletes reach their potential. I am eager to continue with you on the mission of discovering the answers and spreading the word.

INDEX

Note: The italicized *f* following page numbers refers to figures.

ABOUT THE AUTHOR

Cheri Kempf is owner and pitching instructor at Club K, the largest indoor training facility for female fastpitch softball players in the country. She has taught and trained thousands of athletes at Club K since 1991. Best known for her pitching expertise, she was a member of a five-person panel assembled by the Amateur Softball Association (ASA) and the United States Olympic Committee to develop universal standards by which to teach fast-pitch pitching.

Kempf has more than 30 years of experience playing and coaching softball at all levels. In college, Kempf was a three-time All-American, an NAIA Collegiate national champion, and a National Tournament MVP in 1982 with a tournament ERA of 0.00. She then spent four seasons with the world-renowned Raybestos Brakettes, where her team was the ASA Women's Major Level national champion in 1991 and 1992. In 1992 Kempf joined the United States national team and went on to win the gold medal in the World Cup in Beijing, China.

Kempf has been inducted into the NAIA Collegiate Hall of Fame, the Missouri State ASA Hall of Fame, and the Missouri Western State College Hall of Fame. A member of the Women's Sports Foundation and the NFCA, she has done extensive motion analysis research with some of the top biomechanists in the country and has coached softball for four years at the NCAA Division I level. She also invented the Spin Right Spinner, a training device used to teach the correct mechanics of the pitching movement to softball and baseball pitchers, and an indoor three-on-three softball game called "RIPS," which is played with a specially designed cage and fitted to indoor competition.

Kempf lives in Hermitage, Tennessee. Her favorite leisure-time activities are boating, traveling, and visiting her family in Missouri.